Nirala Series
WILDLIFE IN NEPAL

Rishikesh Shaha (1925 —) is Nepal's internationally known political analyst, a veteran statesman, an avid shikari and a conservationist. During his eventful life, he has held several key positions and has authored many books, most noted being , *Modern Nepal : A Political History (1969-1995) Politics in Nepal (1980-1990)*, and *Three Decades and Two Kings : Eclipse of Nepal's Partyless Monarchic Rule in Nepal.*

Currently, Shaha lives in Kathmandu where he works as President of Human Rights Organization of Nepal.

Richard M. Mitchell (1940—), a well known American zoologist, is considered an authority an high altitude Asian mammals. Mitchell has spent more than three decade conducting wildlife researches in Alaska, Canada, China, Egypt, India, Nepal, New Guinea, Pakistan, Sri Lanka , Tibet, and the continental United States. He was awarded a Ph.D. in Zoology from Iowa State University for his research on the accounts of Nepalese mammals and analysis of the Host-Ectoparasite data by computer techniques. He has been employed as a professional big-game guide both in Alaska (1960-63) and Nepal (1965-1970). He has conducted ecological and population surveys of polar bears in Hudson Bay, tigers in Nepal and upland and small game in Ontario, Canada. He was personally invited to the People's Republic of China in 1980, 1982, and 1985. Mitchell has also conducted research on the high altitude mammals in the "Roof Top of the World" (Tibet).

Since 1979, he has been employed by the U.S. Fish and Wildlife Services working for the office of Endangered Species (Federal Assistance Program) and the office of Scientific Authority (Research Program).

Nanda Shumsher J.B. Rana is a leading Nepalese Photographer specialising in the area of wildlife. His works have appeared in distinguished magazines at home and abroad.

NIRALA SERIES

Wildlife in Nepal

Rishikesh Shaha
Richard M.Mitchell

With Colour Plates by
Nanda Shumsher J.B. Rana

Nirala

Nirala Publications
2595 Kucha Challan
Darya Ganj, New Delhi 110 002.

First Edition 2001

ISBN-81-85693-31-5

Cover Design : Uday Shankar

Email:nirala32@hotmail.com

Typesetting at
Micro Tech Printage
Darya Ganj, New Delhi

Printed at
Chaman Offset
New Delhi-2

S.P., Narendra Kazi and Trailokyajee, the late Karki of Manara and other friends and guides-in pleasant memory of many happy days spent together in the hunting camp and the forest. Also in memory of the late Captain Jai Singh (Mamasaheb) whose intense love for Nepal and its people will live forever.

—The Authors

"Never in 100,000 years can I tell you the glories of the Himalaya."

-Upnishad

"We don't inherit the earth from our forefathers; we borrow it from our children."

-Old Chinese Proverb

A full grown male tiger ▶

Centre Spread : A tiger at ease

◄ *A growling tiger*

Preface

to Notes on Hunting and Wildlife Conservation (1970)

Nepal has a wonderful heritage and natural resource in forests and wild life. I have been privileged to experience in these forests the thrill of meeting tigers at close range, of hearing the shama warbling at dawn and admiring the orange beauty of the Flame-of-the-Forest trees.

From time to time, for my personal enjoyments I have jotted down memories in my camp notebook and it is only on the insistence of my hunting friends that I now publish some of them in this book form.

... I belatedly requested Dr. Robert Fleming and his son Dr. R. Fleming, Jr. to correct the scientific and other errors in the book. Had it not been for their valuable assistance, the book would not have been published in its present form. I am grateful to the Flemings for their help. However, the views expressed in the book are entirely my own and I am responsible for all the lapses in the work.

Rishikesh Shaha

15 August 1970 Kathmandu

◄ *A female hog deer at rest*

Preface

Nepal has a wonderful heritage and natural resource in wildlife and forests. In 1965, I first visited this unique Himalayan Kingdom and then spent the next four years living and trekking throughout the country. During this time, I was fortunate to meet Rishikesh Shaha, a leading statesman and an avid shikari (hunter) and conservationist.

Rishi has been privileged to explore the jungles of the tarai, and ``experience the thrill of meeting tigers at close range, of hearing the Shama warbling at dawn, and admiring the orange beauty of the Flame-of-the Forest trees". From time to time, Rishi jotted down his memories in his field notebook, and it is upon his insistence that we are publishing his notes in book form.

The following pages contain brief descriptions and anecdotes on the wildlife along with the current efforts being undertaken to preserve this precious resource. Much of this information is based on field observations made by Rishi and myself, plus excerpts from his book, *Notes on Hunting and Wildlife Conservation in Nepal.* Other information has been borrowed from naturalists whose writings have added much to the sum of knowledge on the wildlife of Nepal. Among the books consulted were:

Blanford, W.T.1891, *The Fauna of British India including Ceylon and Burma.*

Bolton, M.1976, *Royal Karnali Wildlife Reserve Management Plan 1976-1981.*

Borradaile, L.M.Green, L.Morn, P.Robinson, and A.Tait. 1977, *Langtang National Park Management Plan 1977-1982.*

Ellerman, J.R. and T.C.S. Morrison-Scott. 1966. *Checklist of Palaearctic and Indian Mammals, 1958 to 1946.*

Fleming, R.L. Sr., R.L. Fleming, Jr., and L.S.Bangdel, 1976, *Birds of Nepal.*

Gee, E.P.1964, *The Wildlife of India.*

Hagen, T. 1961, Nepal.

Mitchell, R.M. 1977, *Accounts of Nepalese Mammals and Analysis of the Host-Ectoparasite Data by Computer Techniques (Ph.D.Thesis).*

Prater, S.H.1965, *The Book of Indian Mammals.*

Shaha, R.1970, *Notes on Hunting and Wildlife Conservation in Nepal.*

I hope that this book will aid in giving one a brief glimpse of the past hunting history, the present status of wildlife, and the future for the preservation of these unique life forms in Nepal. We must try to preserve what is left of Nepal's forests and the wildlife that inhabits them. The authors record their deep indebtedness to Mr. B.N. Upreti, Director of Department of Wildlife for his substantial help in preparing this edition.

Our ability to publish this work is largely due to the support of the late Mrs. Siddhanta Shaha. We wish to thank Marleen S. Mitchell who kindly typed, read through the manuscript, and offered valuable advice and suggestions.

Richard M.Mitchell
Office of the Scientific Authority U.S. Fish and Wildlife Service Formerly: Office of Endangered Species U.S. Fish and Wildlife Service

Washington, D.C.

Contents

A sloth bear ▶

A grey langur ▶

Centre Spread : A female gaur

Introduction

◄ *A male spotted deer*

Nepal, lying along the slopes of the mighty Himalaya, stretches from east to west and lies between 80^0 and 88^0 East Longitude. Barely a hundred miles wide and stretching from 26^0 to 36^0 North Latitude, its altitudes range from a few feet above sea level to the highest point on earth. Nepal is a land of contrast, ranging from the lowland malarious jungles of the tarai to the barren, windswept, majestic peaks of the Greater Himalayan Mountain chain. This tiny Himalayan Kingdom is shaped like an elongated rectangle, 800 kilometers (km) long, 160 to 240 km wide, and has a total area of about 141,000 km (square kilometers). Nepal is divided broadly into three regions: the Lowlands, Midlands, and Highlands.

The Lowlands include the tarai, bhabar, Chure hills, duns, and the Mahabharat range up to 915 meters (m) or 3,000 feet (ft). The Midlands cover the Mahabharat Lekh (Range) above 915 m as well as the "Middle Hills" or Pahar zone that extend up to 2,745 m (9,000 ft). The Highlands include all of Nepal over 2,745 m.

However, for ecological reasons it can be put in the following six divisions, bisected in the centre by River Kali Gandaki.

1. The Tarai and Bhabar
2. The Churiya hills (Siwaliks)
3. The Mahabharat
4,. The Middle Hills
5. The Main Himalayan Range
6. The Trans-Himalayan Range

The Lowlands

The tarai comprises the northern extension of the Gangetic Plain and is a narrow belt of well-watered alluvial soils stretching from the Indian border northward to the first slopes of the *bhabar*. The tarai was once heavily forested and contained many large mammals and birds. Today, only a small portion of the original tarai forests remain protected in national parks and reserves. His Majesty's Government (HMG) has established national parks and reserves in Suklaphanta and Bardia in the west, in Chitawan and Parsa in the Central and in Koshi Tappu in the east to preserve the unique forms of Nepali wildlife and plants of the tarai.

The tropical deciduous forests of the tarai are divided into three major types: uniform Sal (Shorea robusta), riverine, and mixed forest. While little extensive forest remains in the tarai, considerable Sal growth exists in the *bhabar*. The bhabar is a gently sloping, very dry strip of land between the tarai and Chure or Siwalik hills. The water table is low and consists of mostly gravels and boulders.

The chain of Chure hills rises out of the Gangetic plain and varies from 300 to 1,200 m (1,000-4,000 ft) in elevation. These hills form the outermost range of the Himalaya and are most famous for their Pleistocene mammal deposits. A large number of streams originate in the siwaliks, and the foot hills are clothed with Sal and long-leafed pine.

Between the Chure hill chain to the south and the Mahabharat range to the north lies a series of geosynclinal troughs or longitudinal valleys called duns (pronounced "doons"). The intensively cultivated Dang Dun in the west and the partially forested Rapti Dun (Chitawan Valley) in central Nepal are the best known. The Rapti Dun is one of the largest broad, relatively flat valleys found in Nepal. Two major rivers, the Reu and Rapti, drain southwestward through the Reu-Rapti Valley, joining the Narayani River, which is known as Great Gandak River in India. The vegetative pattern in the Rapti Valley, as in the tarai, reflects the high degree of human disturbance. Bordering the rivers, tall elephant grasses form another unique vegetative type.

The Midlands

The Midlands, in which Kathmandu Valley lies, is situated between the Mahabharat to the south and the Highlands to the north. The oak-rhododendron crowned crests of the Mahabharat Lekh rise to about 2,745 m (9,000 ft.) immediately north of the Chure hills and duns or the inner tarai. The lower slopes of the Mahabharat support dense populations of humans and the hillsides have been totally denuded from centuries of intensive farming (terracing) and overgrazing. Villages cling precariously to mountain sides while terraced fields spread endlessly beneath the houses. By intermittent or continual grazing of livestock, gathering of vegetation for fuel or fodder, and cultivating the hillsides, man has totally modified this life zone and its environment.

The inhospitable highlands to the north and the malarious jungles of the tarai, duns, and bhabar to the south have concentrated the majority of Nepal's population in the Midlands. Many species of plants and animals have been totally eliminated.

The Highlands

Abruptly, the Highlands rise north of the Midlands, forming a steep, rugged barrier along Nepal's northern border. Vegetation on the southern slopes of the Highlands resembles that of the Mahabharat to about 3,000 m (10,000 ft.); then temperate, wet forests of rhododendron-juniper replace the mixed hardwood-pine stands. Rivers have eroded wide valleys, running east and west and parallel to the strike of the Greater Himalayas in the Highlands. From west to east, these large valleys are: Humla, Mugu, Langu, Thakkhola, Manang, Kutang, Kyirong, Rongshar, Khumbu, and Karma. They range in elevation from 2,400-5,000 m (7,500-16,500 ft.).

The timberline varies somewhat, averaging about 3,965 m (13,000 ft.). Local people do not live permanently above tree line, but a few hardy mammals and birds do—Himalayan tahr, snow leopards, blue sheep, mouse-hares (pikas), along with snow cocks and Impeyan pheasants. Above the Himalayan meadows arises a bleak but dramatic land of rocks, snow, and ice. Little life is sustained here.

Summer is the time to visit the Highlands. Birds abound amid the broad carpets of mosses and wild-flowers, and pikas scurry about the boulder heaps, busy preparing their winter stacks of hay. Few people outside local yak herders venture into these Highland meadows because the route is hampered by slippery trails wet from monsoon rains, swollen streams, and voracious leeches clinging to each bit of dwarf vegetation. The area is hostile to the outsiders because of high altitude sickness.

North of the Greater Himalayan Range, in the districts of Dolpo, Mustang and Manang, one enters a high alpine desert. Reduced rainfall combined with high altitude allow Tibetan species to flourish here—woody hares, sand foxes, Himalayan marmots, and Tibetan lynxes. The vegetation is sparse—a combination of Caragana, Lonicera spiny legumes, and stunted rhododendrons, willows and junipers.

A pond heron or a paddy bird▸

A female rhino ▸

Centre Spread : A Gaur

CHAPTER ONE

Past Hunting in Nepal

◄ *Common langurs resting*

Nepal has always been famous for shikar (big game hunting). During the British rule in India, viceroys and governors-general with their entourages, at the invitation of the Rana Prime Ministers, would frequently hunt in the Nepal tarai. These hunts were always laid out in a regal fashion and usually resulted in impressive bags of wildlife: tigers, leopards, rhinos, wild boar, crocodiles, and many numbers of chital (spotted deer) and sambar. Bird shooting was also very popular, and scores of partridges, jungle fowl, and peacocks were shot for the table and for sport.

These hunts usually took place during the winter months, and stalking game was next to impossible since the tarai forests were overgrown with tall elephant grasses. Therefore, most shooting was done from elephant back which gave the hunter the advantage of locating game plus afforded him personal safety.

When Queen Elizabeth and Prince Philip of the United Kingdom visited Nepal in 1961, a royal hunt was laid out at Megauli, Chitawan District, and some 400 elephants were gathered for the occasion. Although the Queen and Prince Philip did not actively take part in the shoot, Lord Hume and Rear Admiral Bonham Carter bagged a rhino and tiger respectively.

The Queen and her husband were not the only members of British or European Royalty to have hunted in Nepal. In 1870, the Duke of Edinburgh, the second son of Queen Victoria, came for a shoot in farwestern Nepal tarai. In 1876, the Prince of Wales (later King Edward VII), shot in same hunting block (from February 16 to March 5), and he bagged 23 tigers, 1 leopard, and several wild boar. Even in those days, the one-horned rhino had been extirpated from the western tarai. Seven tigers were shot in a single day.

In 1911 (from December 16-28), King George V hunted in Sukibhar and Kasra in Chitawan District. The King and suite bagged 39 tigers, 18 rhinos, and 4 sloth bears of which 21 tigers, 8 rhinos, and 1 bear fell to King George's rifle. The record bag for one day was 10 tigers, 1 rhino, and 1 bear.

In 1921, the Prince of Wales (later King Edward VIII), hunting from Thori Camp in Chitawan, shot 17 tigers, 10 rhinos, 2 leopards, and 2 bears. The better-known U.S. big game hunters who have shot in the jungles of Nepal include: Maurice Stans, the former Secretary of Commerce; Byron Engle, retired Director, office of Public Safety, U.S Agency for International Development. Herb Klein and Toddie Wynne, Jr., wealthy Texan oil magnets; and Big John Coapman, a character unto himself. The late King Mahendra was a keen shikari and a great lover of sport shooting himself.

In 1959, John Coapman opened the first professional hunting company in Nepal. Chalak sleek (smart) as a tiger and ruthless as a leopard, Big John later turned his efforts to the conservation of wildlife and opened up a tourist lodge, Tiger Tops Hotel, near Megauli in Chitawan. Here tourists could shoot tigers and wildlife with Nikons, Minoltas, and the like. Tiger Tops Hotel has provided a source of hard currency for the government and has yielded insurmountable pleasure and entertainment to tourists and wildlife enthusiasts the world over.

In the past, it was impossible to hunt in Nepal except at the invitation of His Majesty's Government (HMG). But times changed and selected areas were opened to big game hunting all except for rhinos, gaur (bison), and wild buffalo. Big game hunting and poaching has taken their toll of Nepal's natural treasure—its wildlife. Also, with the advent of malaria eradication (1956), starving hill peoples moved into the luxuriant jungles of the tarai, slashing and burning the pristine hardwood forests and turning the grassy expanses under to the plough. Elephant grass was cut for thatch, and illegal timber activities pruned the Sal forests. Today, little of the original Tarai forests remain intact.

The "horn of plenty" has run out. No less than 35 species of mammals are endangered and 15 big game species face possible extinction within the next decade. Already the pygmy hog and wild yak have disappeared and the last report of these two unique animals occurring in Nepal was in the early 1950's. The tiger has been reduced to less than a few hundred in number. Less than 400 rhinos are restricted to the Reu-Rapti Valley. The magnificent black buck antelope numbers less than 150 in the agricultural land in Bardia. And the wild buffalo, numbering less than 50, is found only in the floodplain of the Sapta Kosi.

Swamp deer, which used to congregate in herds of thousands, are now reduced to small herds frequenting the marshy Shukla Phanta of western Nepal. The late King Mahendra was aware of this alarming rate of disappearance of his country's wildlife, and he instituted a series of national parks and reserves to try to preserve the species.

CHAPTER TWO

Nepal's Famous Ring Method of Hunting

Tiger ! ▶

Centre Spread : Tiger and a cub

In the past, the ring method was employed for hunting tigers and leopards because it was one of the surest methods of bagging these wily and uncanny beasts. In organizing a ring shoot, large numbers of elephants were required, and in the old days as many as 600 elephants would be assembled for a "Royal" shoot.

The first night of the hunt, buffalo calves were staked out as "bait" in preselected areas of the jungle. The following morning, trackers would set out on foot to locate any buffalo kills and would then track the tiger to his suspected resting place. A tiger usually makes a kill, then drags the carcass to a secluded spot and gorges himself. When satisfied with the meal the tiger will den up close by to protect his spoil from jackals, hyaenas, and vultures. The trackers follow the pug marks (footprints) and closely examine the layout to make sure that the tiger is still in the vicinity of the kill.

Cutting the Circle

The footprints will reveal to them whether it is a big or small tiger or one or several. They also carefully examine the drag or the direction taken. They then quietly proceed on foot and make a large circle of a quarter to a half mile diameter, marking out the circumference

◀A tiger over a wild boar kill

with chipped stems and grass knots as they go, and trying to make sure that the drag has not gone beyond the circle. If the drag is found to have gone beyond the circle, they make another circle. The idea is to have the circle enclose the end of the drag. This is called ``cutting the circle" by the shikaris and the final circle makes the future ``Ring".

Completing the Circuit

Once the ring was cut, then the elephants were sent for. The elephants were then divided into two groups which proceeded very quietly in single file right and left along the perimeter of the outer circle. The rear elephants gradually drop out to take their positions at regular intervals, and finally the two lead elephants meet. The word is then passed down both sides that the circuit is completed, "lam pugyo," which is immediately followed by the command "mudi phira" -turn the heads inwards.

Closing the Ring

Now the whole circle of elephants move inward crushing the grasses and bushes. The mahoots, mounted on the elephants, shout and whistle to drive the tiger towards the center. The circle becomes smaller and smaller until the elephants are almost touching each other. The tiger is surrounded by a solid wall of elephants, leaving less than a half mile of territory to seek refuge in.

Spreading a Sheet of White Linen

Once the ring is formed, a winding sheet of white

linen is spread around the circle and propped up with branches and limbs. This ring or purdah of white cloth-which, as experience has proven, is by itself sufficient to keep the tiger within the circle. The sudden appearance of this white cloth fluttering in the breeze scares the tiger making it reluctant to jump the ring. Now the elephants are freed to ring another tiger within the immediate vicinity. Thus ringing made it possible to hunt and shoot several tigers in one day. This ingenious method of using a winding sheet of white linen to ring a tiger was first employed by the late Field Marshall Rudra Shamsher Jang Bahadur Rana.

Beating for the Tiger

Once the ring was secure, beater elephants were sent in to trample the remaining underbrush to flush the tiger or tigers from their hiding places. Many times several tigers were trapped in the same ring. Then the message was sent back to camp, and the V.I.P.'s arrived in howdahs on elephant back. Now the tigers were driven by the beater elephants toward an opening in the ring and shot by the hunters from the howdahs.

Following is a vivid and dramatic description of ring-shooting of tigers from *Big-game Shooting in Nepal* by E.A. Smythies. ``Glimpses of one or more slinking forms are seen in the grass and undergrowth, when suddenly a tiger breaks cover and charges with a roar, to be met by volleys of shots or shouts or missiles if he charges the ring. Backwards and forwards it dashes looking for a way or means of escape, to a pandemonium of men shouting and elephants trumpeting, grumbling and gurgling, thumping their trunks on the ground, and occasionally, when directly charged, turning tail and bolting in terror.

``Normally, a tiger does not attack a man or an elephant, but once it is cornered it becomes a fighting animal of diabolical fury, utterly fearless of man or elephant, whom it attacks in a mad rage without a moment's hesitation. It has been known to reach a machan about 15 feet high up in a tree and hurl a hunter out of his perch or machan, it has been seen to leap a height of 15 or 16 feet into a tall howdah and sometimes a tiger will try to break through a ring by charging home on an elephant."

The thrills and dangers of shooting a ringed tiger are not to be minimized. The following excerpt from Wenthworth Day's *King George V as a Sportsman* gives another thrilling account of the excitement and danger that ring-shooting presented. "It is no sport for bad shots, hasty, excitable people, or those with no stomach for danger. Even the most blase hunter is likely to experience for a second or two a sudden spasm of fear when he first hears the blood-curdling roar of an infuriated tiger, and sees the great striped body launched into its charge, a thruderbolt of death and anger in mid-air. It is one of the most terrific sights in the world."

CHAPTER THREE

Some Wildlife of the Lowlands

The Nepal lowlands can boast of exceptional beauty of flaming forests in bloom as well as the unusual diversity of its wildlife. The tarai is rich in mam mal and bird life with no less than 20 big game animals inhabiting its jungles. The beasts of prey are most prevalent (tigers and leopards) with a myriad of smaller carnivores (jackals, foxes, civets, and mongooses) occupying the fringes. The rivers were once infested with gavials, crocodiles, Gangetic dolphins, and otters.

Following is a brief account of some of the mammals of the lowlands, their scientific and common names, and interesting notes from published records and our own personal field observations.

THE CARNIVORES

There is an interdependence and interrelationship among animals living together in a particular area, however varied their species. The organization of an animal community and the relationships maintained between its members center largely on the question of food and its distribution. In the lowlands, there are primary carnivores (tigers, leopards, and wild dogs), the secondary carnivores (lesser cats, foxes, and civets) and the scavengers (hyaenas and jackals).

Tiger (Panthera tigris) - Bagh

"Though supreme in his forests, there is one enemy a tiger must fear and that is another tiger." The tiger is a richly coloured, powerfully built beast that is found throughout the jungles of the tarai. Few tigers exceed 3 m (10 ft.) in length, the average male being 2.5-2.75 m (9-9.5 ft.) with females a little over 2.0 m (8.5 ft.). The average male weighs 180-230 kg (400-500 1b.); females weigh about 45 kg (100 1b.) less.

At the turn of the century, over 50,000 tigers inhabited the jungles and forests of the Indian subcontinent. Now less than 3,000 exist, the number remaining in Nepal is unknown but most likely is less than 300. They once ranged up to 2,300 in the midlands, but their present range is restricted to the dense jungles of the eastern and western tarai and the Rapti dun.

The peak breeding season is from November to February. The gestation period is approximately 90 to 105 days and the young, usually 2-3, but as many as 6, are born between February and May. Cubs remain with the female until they are two years old. Tigers may live up 15 to 16 years in the wild and longer in captivity.

The tiger's method of hunting is based on only a moderate sense of smell, very keen sight and hearing, great physical strength combined with a formidable armament of teeth and claws, protective colouration, the ability to move as silent as a shadow, and great speed in charging. So the tiger works for his living by still-hunting and stalking to within charging distance.

A king vulture ▶

Centre Spread : A crested hog eagle

A tiger follows a fairly regular routine prowling a beat or stretch of territory in search of game. When the tiger makes a kill, it drags the carcass into dense undergrowth to conceal its spoil from other mauraders such as hyaenas, leopards, jackals, and vultures. A tiger can consume vast amounts of meat, up to 30 kg at one time. Then they don't have to feed for several days. Cheetal or spotted deer and sambar are its favorite prey, but driven by hunger a tiger will consume almost anything— fish, fowl, reptiles, and even carrion.

As a rule, tigers are perfect gentlemen and do not attack humans unless provoked or cornered. They only become man-eaters after being wounded or disabled from age or some other natural cause. Man-eaters do not live in or roam the depths of the forest, but move close to human habitation or remain along the forest edge adjoining villages. Sometimes they make their way into villages in search of humans.

It is said that once tigers take to man-eating, they grow lazy and find lying in wait for man much easier than stalking wild animals in the dense forests. Once they acquire the taste for human flesh, they seem to lose the interest in preying on other animals. Man-eaters are generally found to be emaciated, but are much more cunning than the common run of tigers. One tigress took 56 human victims in the western tarai before being dispatched.

Leopard or Panther (Panthera pardus) - Chituwa

When every other wild animal has disappeared from the Nepal jungles, the leopard will persist. This mag-

◀ *A king vulture*

nificent cat is the most devious, cunning and brazen beast found in the tarai. One never knows whether the leopard is going to exhibit great boldness or extreme caution. Leopards are able to live and thrive almost anywhere. They are not restricted to dense forest or heavy cover like tigers but thrive in open country as well as among rocks and scrub.

The typical Nepali leopard is a sleek, short-haired animal with a fulvous or bright fulvous coat marked with black spots or rosettes. The spots on the head are small and more or less rounded, while on the flanks, belly, and outer sides of the legs, the markings become solid black blotches. The long tail is pale yellow with a double row of elongate black spots. An exceptionally large male may reach 2.6 m (8 ft.) in length and weigh 68 kg (200 1b.) They possess amazing strength and can carry a kill one and one-half times their weight up a tree.

Leopards range from the subtropical jungles of the tarai to the coniferous forests of the midlands. They take the path of least resistance, prowling stream beds, foot paths, and jungle roads. Generally nocturnal, they usually hunt alone but sometimes in pairs. Their habits bring them into far more frequent contact with man than the tiger. They are a greater potential scourge on human life and property, preying mainly on goats, calves, sheep, and quite commonly dogs. In winter, leopards are known to enter Kathmandu Valley and prey on dogs and monkeys.

Mating can take place at any time of the year and

a female leopard will come in heat with in a few months of being separated from the cubs and their call, a cross between a grunt and a cough repeated quickly 4-5 times, is prevalent during this time. The gestation period is about 13 weeks and 2-4 young are born in February and March.

Sloth Bear (Melursus ursinus) - Bhalu

The sloth bear has a coarse, shaggy, black coat often mixed with brown. The fur is longest between the shoulders, and the chest marking, typically V-or Y-shaped, varies from dirty white to yellow. The muzzle is elongated and the lower lip protrudes. The hind legs are short and the feet are equipped with long, ivory white claws. A sloth bear may stand 1.4-1.7 m (4.5-5.5 ft.) and weigh up to 145 kg (320 1b.).

Sloth bears inhabit dense, almost impenetrable thickets and ravines overgrown with bramble. These animals are generally nocturnal, although during cool weather they are active throughout the day. Their sense of smell is well-developed, but their eyesight and hearing are poor. Omnivorous in food habit they consume large quantities of fruit, vegetable matter, insects, grubs, honey, bird eggs, and carrion. It is one of the most dangerous animals in the forest and can attack without provocation.

Mating takes place at about the onset of the monsoon rains (late June-early July). The gestation period is about 7 months with young born from October through February-Most often in December or January. One to two cubs are born in a ground shelter and remain with the female until they are nearly full grown, possibly 2-3 years.

Elephant (Elephas maximus) - Hatti

Smaller than the African elephant, the Asian elephant does not have the enormous ears and hollow back of its African cousin. It has four nails on each hindfoot, the African only has three, and the trunk ends in a single "lip" in contrast with two equal-sized "lips" in the African species. Generally, only males have large tusks, the tusks of females barely protrude only a few inches. The ponderous pachyderm stands 2.5-3.0 m high at the shoulders, has a head and body length of 5.5-6.5 m, and weighs about 5,000 kg. Elephants have very poor eyesight, but highly developed senses of smell and hearing.

The elephant chiefly frequents areas covered with tall forests where the ground is hilly or undulating and where bamboo grows in profusion. Gregarious, they roam in herds of 15-25, feeding in the early morning, evening, and at night. Their diet consists of grasses, leaves, tender shoots, fruit, and field crops. Their fondness for sugarcane and paddy raises havoc with local farmers. A full grown elephant will consume 270 to 320 kg (600-700 1b.) of fodder a day.

There seems to be no definite breeding season. The gestation period is 600-650 days (about 22 months) and mostly one and sometimes two young ones are born. Individuals have been known to live over 100 years in captivity and in the wild about 45-60 years.

In Nepal, elephants are rare in the wild. They have been reported from Parsa, Chitawan, Bardia, and Kanchanpur Districts. There is no exact count of wild elephants remaining in Nepal, but the number is probably less than 50.

The Asian elephant has long been captured, domesticated, and used as a transport animal in Nepal, India, Burma, and Thailand. Since these animals don't readily breed in captivity, most work elephants have to be captured and tamed. Until the late 18th century, land tax payable to the British East India Company by Nepal was assessed in terms of elephants.

Different methods are employed in capturing elephants. The palisade method, employed in India and elsewhere, has rarely been used in Nepal. A herd is driven into a funnel-shaped palisade or a strongly built stockade and trapped. A second method used in days gone-by was trapping elephants in pits. It was employed to capture a rogue elephant driven out of its overlordship of the female herd by a younger, more virile tusker. The rogue would usually be in a sexually aroused state (musth) and would be a lone wanderer of the forest-ill-tempered and dangerous.

A pit was dug large and deep enough to accommodate the beast and was carefully camouflaged with earth and grasses and weeds. Then a few well trained female elephants were stationed 40-50 yards away from the pit. Elephants, as a rule, are extremely careful about where they tread, and usually feel the ground with the tips of the trunk at every step before they proceed. But a bull elephant in a state of sexual tumescence loses its sense of caution on sight or scent of females and plunges headlong into the pit.

Another method of capturing elephants is call the "jangi" or war 'kheda" which literally means "the battle chase." A tusker or a herd of wild elephants is chased continuously back and forth by a group of trained elephants throughout the forest for days on end. Even the mighty wild tuskers become so tired that they lag behind allowing themselves to be easily lassoed.

Elephants can maintain a burst of speed only for a short distance so after a chase of a mile or so, the wild tusker turns and prepares for battle. At this point, the female elephants are withdrawn and the big fighting bulls are brought forward for battle. The situation now calls for the greatest pluck and courage on the part of the mahouts (elephant trainers). One bull engages the enraged tusker in a head-on fight with tusks interlocked and writhing trunks intertwined in "Chaudanta" (meaning four tusks together). Meanwhile, other trained elephants push and pommel at the sides of the wild tuskers.

Soon the wild elephant gives up this unequal fight and turns tail. Its pursuit is immediately resumed with the strategy of denying it any rest or respite. Sometimes the pursuit is interrupted by fights which may last two or more days. The struggle is very strenuous and requires experienced and skilled mahouts who are adept at throwing a rope noose around the neck or hind legs of the fleeing tusker.

Once the tusker is lassoed, it is frightened into submission by the charge of trained elephants and blank fire of guns. After a struggle, the wild elephant is subdued, harnessed, and dragged by the trained elephants into camp. Sometimes, the wild elephant has to be shot in the legs with buckshot before it is subdued in the manner described above.

By careful training, these wild elephants can be made so docile and obedient to the mahout that they understand all his signals by the prodding of his feet and also carry out all his verbal commands (e.g., "run down to the corner and get me a newspaper."). In Nepal, elephants are trained for hunting and are so well controlled that they can flush partridge or jungle fowl or beat a tiger out of cover. They are even taught to hold their breath so the hunter can take a true aim and shoot accurately.

Fighting wild tuskers with trained elephants used to be a great sport in Nepal. Trained, fleet-footed female elephants were used to lure wild elephants into the open where skilled sportsmen and experienced mahouts would be waiting on their trusted tuskers to challenge the wild bulls when they charged the females. After a trying and thrilling fight, which lasted for hours, the wild elephants were either made to retreat or were lassoed and captured when they become completely exhausted. Maharaj Jang Bahadur, the founder of the administrative system of the hereditary Rana Prime Ministers in Nepal, was very fond of fighting wild tuskers.

On his way home from England in 1850, Jang

Bahadur stopped in Ceylon to worship at the Temple of Rameshwaram to purge himself of any sin or impurity that he might have acquired on his visit to Europe. It was here that he met and befriended Laurence Oliphant, son of the then Chief Justice of Ceylon. The young Irishman, full of vigour and enterprise, was so attracted by the prospects for adventure, hunting, and sport that he accompanied the Maharaj on his return trip to Nepal.

Oliphant left his impressions of his adventures in a book, *A Journey to Kathmandu.* He was the first Westerner to witness this breath-taking sport of fighting and capturing wild elephants: "Taking off my shoes and tying a towel round my head, I was told to suppose an immense branch to be in front of me, and was taught to escape its sweeping effects by sliding down the crupper of the elephant, and keeping the whole of my body below the level of his back, thus allowing the branch to pass within an inch above without touching me. In the same manner, upon a branch threatening me from the right or left, it was necessary to throw myself on the opposite side, hanging only by my hands, and swinging myself into my original position by a most violent exertion, which required at the same time considerable knack. Having perfected myself in these accomplishments to the upmost of my power, I awaited in patience the arrival of the elephants."

From the above, it is clear that fighting wild elephants was for the stouthearted and the able-bodied and the participant needed a high standard of physical fitness, acrobatic skill, along with a constant presence of mind and will to meet the risks and thrills of this

Orange Punch▶
Centre Spread : A butterfly sucking nectar

sport.

Though capturing wild elephants was great sport and venture for daring men like Jang Bahadur, in more recent times, His Majesty's Government (HMG) has acquired the sole monopoly of catching elephants. The government used to organize at least one or two "khedas" annually in order to maintain the Royal herd of elephants. As it is an endangered species, no more capturing or killing is permitted at present.

The Great Asian One-Horned Rhinoceros (Rhinoceros unicornis) - Gaida

The Great Asian one horned rhinoceros is a large, awkward-looking creature with a big head, short, stumpy limbs, small eyes, and wide nostrils with prehensile lips. It has a single "horn" on the upper surface of the nose which is composed of agglutinated hairs and has no firm attachment to the bones of the skull. The skin which is covered with large convex tubercles, has a number of loose folds, giving the animal the appearance of wearing armour. Contrary to popular belief, rhinos use their sharply pointed lower tusks rather than the horn for defense. The length of the head and body is 2.1-4.2 m, the height at the shoulders 1.3-20 m, and the weight 2,000-4,000 kg.

Formerly, the rhino inhabited the grasslands of the entire tarai, but presently it is restricted to an area of about 1,000 sq. km of the Rapti and Reu River Valleys in Chitawan and Nawal Parasi Districts. Preferring swampy ground, they frequent uncultivated alluvial plains in the Rapti. They are more or less solitary, but several animals may occupy the same tract of dense vegetation. Their diet consists of grasses, reeds, and young shoots, and they are also fond of paddy (rice). The gestation period is approximately 19 months; a single calf is born between February and April. Their life span in the wild may exceed 50 years.

Past surveys have documented the decline of this species in Nepal and only 350 to 400 animals remain. Habitat destruction and poaching have drastically reduced their numbers. Powdered rhino horn is sold as an "aphrodisiac", and a kilogram of horn will bring upwards of $20,000 U.S. in Hong-Kong and Taiwan.

Poachers take advantage of the rhino's peculiar habit of defecating in the same area. Once poachers discover such a deposit of fresh excreta, they dig a pit in front of the dung heap wide enough to hold a rhino and deep enough to prevent it from scrambling out. Then the poachers prepare a trellis of twigs, branches, and sticks and spread a thin layer of earth over the network. The purpose is to deceive the rhino, which is dull of sight, into believing it is on normal hard ground. When the rhino backs up to defecate on its dung heap as is its usual practice, it crashes into the pit. With the rhino imprisoned, the poachers hack off its horn with an axe, and sometimes they kill the animal for its meat. The pit method is popular among poachers because it does not employ the use of firearms that might alert the forest guards. The usual method of poaching is by shooting but now-a-days poison is also used in baiting (in field).

Ring-shooting was never suited for hunting rhinos because all they had to do was charge the ring to break it in confusion. Elephants, timid in nature, are easily upset by even the sight of small animals such as porcupines—the rhino is ``facile princeps". Most elephants flee at the mere glimpse of rhino and hence the staunchest elephants are needed to tackle them.

Wild Boar (Sus scrofa) - Badel

The wild boar is characterized by a long head and a long snout that has a rounded terminal pad for rooting. The first two upper incisors are broad and laterally compressed; the third incisor is small. The canines (tusks) curve outward and upward in both jaws. Record measurements of lower tuskers are 32 cm. (12:5/8 in.) on the outside curve. Large males may weigh in excess of 230 kg. (500 1bs.).

Widely distributed in Nepal, the wild boar ranges from the scanty bush jungle of the tarai, throughout the oak forests in the Midlands, into the alpine meadows of the Highlands. In Langtang Valley, a wild boar was sighted at an altitude of 4,500 m. (14,500 ft.).

Wild boars are generally nocturnal, resting in undergrowth or thickets during the day. They travel in herds of 10-12, and sometimes up to 50 are found together. Omnivorous, they root for roots and tubers, and they do extensive damage to grain crops and fields of potatoes. They have also been known to feed on carrion.

Females have 1-2 litters of 3-8 piglets annually with a reported gestation period of 112-115 days. The piglets display a characteristic striped coat consisting of a median black strips with an ochereous stripe beginning laterally at the nape. This striped pattern alternates laterally, breaking up into spots on the haunches. Piglets are born between May and August.

Females have the habit of building a nest for reception of the young. The nest, usually hollowed in a hillside, is lined with grasses and is covered over with stems and twigs. Males also have the habit of constructing a nest. They can be highly dangerous and there have been cases where in a fight with a tiger, the tiger has died.

Pygmy Hog (Sus salvanius) - Bam-pudke Badel

Hardly 25 cm. (10 in.) at the shoulders, and weighing only 4-5 kg. (10-12 1bs.), the pygmy hog once inhabited the Sal forests at the base of the Himalayas in Nepal, Sikkim, Bhutan, and Assam. The scarcity of sightings since 1900 led experts to believe that the pygmy hog was extinct, but in 1971, 14 adults and 4 young were captured in Assam by natives while fleeing the flames of a forest fire.

Since pygmy hogs are nocturnal and inhabit the dense elephant grass complex they could still be present in the western tarai and Rapti Dun.

Cheetal or Spotted Deer (Axis axis) - Cheetal

The cheetal is perhaps the most beautiful deer in the world. The coat is a bright, rufous fawn covered with white spots and with white underparts. A dark stripe runs from the nape to the tail, bordered along the back by 1 or 2 rows of white spots. Males have long, 3 tined antlers (up to 100 cm. or 39 in.) and weigh up to 85 kg. (190 1bs.). Cheetals are found in the Sal forests and open grasslands of the tarai and duns, usually in herds of 10 to 20, but sometimes in excess of 100 animals.

They usually begin feeding in early evening and eat until about mid-morning before taking to cover. They feed both on grasses and browse but prefer green vegetation and cultivated crops such as rape (mustard) and wheat. They are somewhat limited in their movements and range, and within a single year a herd may cover a total area of only 15-20 sq. km.

Males shed their antlers in September and October, and new antlers are usually in velvet only until the end of December. Rut begins in March, and mating takes place during April and May. The gestation period is 8-8.5 mo. and fawns are dropped in late January and early February. Usually a single fawn is born and rarely twins. Cheetals are the favorite prey of the tiger. When alarmed, they utter a sharp bark which is repeated several times. A tiger cannot outrun a cheetal, and when these deer spot a tiger in the Jungle, they sound their alarm and will then follow the tiger at a safe distance.

Sambar (Cervus unicolor) - jarayo

The sambar is the largest of all Nepali deer, and stags have massive antlers 90-120 cm. (36-45 in.) in length. The three-tined antlers, borne on short pedicles, are shed in December and January. The coat is coarse and shaggy, forming a mane on the nape and throat. During the hot weather, much of the hair is shed. Hinds (females) are generally brown with a grayish tinge in colour, and older stags are dark blue or almost black. The sambar stands nearly 1.5 m. high at the shoulder and weighs 225-320 kg. (500-750 1bs.).

Found in both dry and moist deciduous forests, these deer inhabit the lower foothills of the Churse hills or the Siwalik, and the undulating areas of the tarai and Rapti Dun from 300-1,000 m. Their favourite haunts are the forested (Sal) hillsides preferably near cultivation. During the hot, dry season, sambars love to wallow in mud. They usually occur singly or in pairs, but sometimes as many as 10-15 animals will congregate in a herd. Their food consists of grasses, leaves, and various kinds of wild fruit. They feed mainly at night retiring into heavy brush at daybreak.

Mating takes place in October and November and fawns (1 or 2) are born the following May or June. The gestation period is 230-240 days.

When alarmed, sambars first utter a snorting whistle followed by a sharp, metallic "ponk" which is repeated several times. When irritated, they will enlarge and contract the suborbital glands. Natives believe that sambar enlarge these glands to entrap flies.

Swamp Deer (Cervus duvauceli) - Barasinga

This splendid deer attains its finest development in the grasslands and reed beds along major rivers, swampy areas, and dry and moist deciduous forests of the Western tarai. It has an elongate muzzle, a neck mane and unique antlers. Barasinga, literally translated, means "12 tines or branches." The antlers are somewhat flattened and both the second and third tines are lacking. There are usually 12 tines altogether, though there may be as many as 20.

The summer coat is a bright, rufous brown. Down the middle of the back, there is usually a broad brown stripe, bordered on each side by a row of white spots. The throat, inner sides of the thighs and underparts are white or whitish. The lower surface of the tail is pure white. A good stag stands 135 cm. (54 in.) at the shoulder and weighs 150-200 kg. (350-450 1bs.).

Swamp deer avoid dense jungles, inhabiting alluvial floodplains and swampy lowlands that are covered with tall grasses and sissoo. Formerly, they were widely distributed over the entire western tarai of Nepal; now they are limited to Bardia and Kanchanpur Districts. Swamp deer are highly gregarious, congregating in herds of 300-350. During rut, several hundred animals have been known to gather together. In 1952, Dr. Robert L. Fleming, Sr., reported seeing herds of well over 500 animals in the Bardia District but now it is estimated about 25-30 animals.

Swamp deer feed on grasses and sedges and actively graze throughout the day. Rutting commences in October and stronger stag may gather a harem of as many as 30 females. The gestation period is approximately 6 months.

In Nepal, barasinga has so drastically declined in numbers that the continued existence of the species is in doubt. Destruction of their habitat and poaching have led to this drastic decline. Large areas of the western tarai have been opened up for agriculture, and their reed beds and tall grasses have been cut for thatch. Livestock grazing has destroyed vast stands of grasses along all the major streams. Also, night hunting by jeep and night lighting has led to wholesale slaughter of these magnificent deer. Presently, the largest number of swamp deer are found in the Shuklaphanta Wildlife Reserve, in a large swampy area bordering the Mahakali River. It is estimated about 2000 in number.

Four-horned Antelope (Tetracerus quadricoinis) - Chausingha or Chauka

Four-horned antelope differ from all other existing antelope by the presence of 2 pairs of horns in males, of which the first pair is much smaller than the second. The horns are short, conical, and smooth. Chausinghas are somewhat similar in appearance to barking deer. The colour is a dull, pale brown with a more or less rufous tinge on the back. There is a dark blackish brown stripe down the front of each leg. The muzzle and outer surface of the ears are blackish. Old bucks measure about 65 cm. (25 in.) at the shoulder and weigh 15-20 kg. (35-45 1b.).

Chausinghas inhabit hilly terrain of the western and eastern tarai, seeking shelter in dense grasses and heavy thickets. They are reported seen in southern side of RCNP in Madi area. They are found in Parsa WR also.

They are shy creatures that move with a peculiar, jerky gait. They usually occur singly and have the habit of defecating in one place. Mating takes place during the monsoons (July through September) and the young are born in January or February. The gestation period is approximately 180 days, the litter size is 1-2.

Blue Bull (Boselaphus tragocamelus) - Nilgai or Ghod Gada

The nilgai is the largest antelope that is native to the tarai. Old bulls may weigh up to 225 kg. (500 1bs.). The head is long and pointed, the forelegs are somewhat longer than the hind legs, and the tail is long. Both sexes have neck manes, and males have a tuft of hair or a "bell" on the throat. Bulls are iron gray in colour and the underside is white. The throat tuft and tail are black. The female is smaller with the iron gray areas of the male replaced by tawny fawn. Only the bulls have short, stout conical horns.

Old males are often solitary, but occasionally they associate in herds. Females and young, together with one or more males, usually make up a herd. They frequent the open grassy plains and dry scrub feeding throughout the day and also at night. They also have the habit of defecating in the same spot and large dung heaps accumulate. Nilgai can gallop at a considerable speed and for quite a distance. Two bulls were clocked at a top speed of 56 km. per hour (42 mph.).

These ungainly looking creatures were for long afforded protection from hunting through their name only. Nilgai means "blue bull" and local shikaris, thinking that they were members of the cow family, would not shoot nilgai due to their religious convictions against killing cows. But now the situation has changed and the species is becoming endangered. Mating takes place during March and April, and 1-2 young are born about 8 months later (240-245 days).

Black Buck Antelope (Antelope cervicapra)-Barat or Krishna Sar

The graceful black buck is the most striking and beautiful of all antelope. Old bucks have horns that twist in a corkscrew- like spiral and may reach 65 cm. (25 in.) in length. An average good buck will stand about 30 cm. in height in shoulder and will weight about 36 kg. (80 lbs.) Black bucks are one of the few antelopes in which diomorphism in sex is significant. (the colouration of males differs significantly from that of females) Females and young males are yellowish brown on the back with a white belly. Old bucks are blackish brown or black except on the nape, which is rufous brown, while the sides of the neck and face are blackish brown except for a white area around each eye. The underparts are white. These two colours (dorsal and ventral) are sharply delineated.

Black buck inhabit open plains, avoiding heavy jungles or hilly terrain. They are somewhat nocturnal, spending the heat of the day in dense scrub thickets, Usually they are found in herds of 20-30, although there are reports from India that several hundred gather together at one time. Only 20 years ago these animals were abundant in the plains and open forests of Banke and Bardra Districts. Heavy poaching, hunting by jeeps, and agriculture encroachment has resulted in their almost total disappearance from Nepal. At present about 150 animals are surviving in agricultural land near Gulariya in Bardia.

In March, when the fruits of the maua tree (Bassia latifolia) are falling like rain, the blackbucks congregate to feed on the fallen spoils. When alarmed they "prong" or spring into the air. First one member of the herd springs into the air, then another and another and finally they turn tail and flee. Their diet consists of grasses, cereal grains and fruit. They breed in late March through early May and 1 to 2 fawns are born after a gestation period of about 180 days.

Kalidas, the world famous Sanskrit poet and dramatist, in an exquisite stanza of verse in his best-known drama, *Shakutala,* graphically describes a black buck being pursued by the hunter in a chariot who happens to be no less a person than King Dushyanta, the hero of the play itself. The quatrain is so vivid and poignant that it helps the reader visualise the scene in mind with every pictorial detail: "The black buck in flight looks beautiful as it turns its back again and again to cast its glance at the pursuing chariot, with the hind part of its body also entered or slumped into its forepart for fear of being hit by arrows. With its path being littered with half-chewed Drava or Duvo grass falling from its mouth agape with fatigue, looks at the back, which while leaping forward moves most of the time in the air and scarcely over the ground." Anyone who has seen a black buck bouncing in the air with all of its four feet together will at once appreciate the accuracy of the above description.

The quatrain in Sanskrit runs as follows:

ग्रीवाभङ्गाभिरामं मुहरनुपर्तात स्यन्दने दन्तवृष्टिः।
पश्चार्द्धेन प्रविष्टः शरपतनमयात् भूयसा पूर्वकायम्।।
दर्भैरर्द्धावलीढैः श्रमविवृतखभ्रंशिभिः किर्णवतर्नां।
पश्योद ग्रल्पत्वात् बहुतंर स्तोकमुर्यां प्रयाति।।

Gaur or Bison (Bos gaurus)- Guari Gai

With a huge head, deep, massive body and stout limbs, the gaur is the embodiment of terror and strength. Standing 5-6 ft. at the shoulders, weighing upwards of 2,000 lbs. (900 kg.), and having massive horns (40 in.) that are flattened at the base and curving strongly inward with inclined tips, it is one of the heaviest bovines in the world. Even the tiger avoids conflict with the gaur. The nearly hairless bodies of old bulls are jet black with whitish muzzles and white stockings. There is a prominent dorsal ridge or hump that begins between the withers and ends abruptly in the middle of the back.

They inhabit the undisturbed tracts of the hill sal forests, the tall grasslands, and the moist deciduous forests between 300-1,500 m. Though never plentiful, only a few survive in the eastern tarai, Rapti Dun, and eastern Siwaliks. Poaching, poisoning, and habitat loss have drastically reduced their numbers. The Birganj District Forest Officer reported the poisoning of 9 gaur at Shikari Bas, Parsa District in March 1970.

Gaur prefer the rocky, forested foothills. They are

found in herds of 5 or 6 to as many as 20. Old bulls are solitary. Gaur are shy and avoid agricultural lands, feeding in early morning or late evening. Their food consists chiefly of grasses and they are quite fond of bamboo shoots. They mate during the winter months, with a single calf born the following August or September. The shyness of these animals and the dense undergrowth which they inhabit make it difficult to estimate the number of gaur remaining in Nepal.

Wild Buffalo or Indian Buffalo (Bubalus bubalis)- Arna

The arna is heavily built with the contour of the back nearly straight. A bull may stand 170 cm. at the shoulder and weigh 900 kg. The horns are more or less triangular for the greater part of their length and are situated low on the skull. The spread of the horns in old bulls may approach 275cm. (108 in.) and in cows 197cm.

In Nepal buffaloes exist in the Sunsari District of the eastern tarai. Arna inhabit the many islands, sand bars, and swamp of the Sapta Kosi River floodplain in eastern Nepal. They feed during the morning and evening, spending the heat of the day in mud wallows or water holes. They feed strictly on grasses.

They are very similar in appearance to the tame buffalo and often breed with them. Destruction of their habitat, hybridization with tame buffaloes, and poaching has reduced their numbers to less than 50 in all of Nepal. Their future looks bleak, and one outbreak of rinderpest, a disease of domestic livestock, could completely finish this small herd in Nepal. Moreover, the rise in the water level of the Kosi Reservoir as a result of the closing of Barrage gates to protect land on the Indian side from being inundated causes concern for the safety and survival of wild buffalo.

They mate near the end of monsoons (September) and the gestation period is approximately 10 months. Usually one calf is born the following summer (June or July).

CHAPTER FIVE

Some Wildlife of the Midlands

A python swallowing up a medium sized spotted deer ▶

Centre Spread : A monitor lizard

The Mahabharat Range rises to about 2,745 m. (9,000 ft.) immediately north of the duns and Chure Hills. Standing atop the Mahabharat, one is awed by the waves of blue-hazed ridges which stretch northward to the giant snow peaks of the Greater Himalayan Range. This zone is the Midlands and together with the Mahabharat comprise an area called the Pahar (Middle Hills).

This zone, with elevations varying from 600-4,000 m, is characterized by gentle sloping terrain and a temperate climate. The midlands support the heaviest human populations, and most of the hillsides have been denuded of their forests, heavily grazed, and terraced for farming. The average width of this region is 60-100 km. Much of the original forests of pine, oak, rhododendron and fir have been destroyed and cut for firewood. Much of the original wildlife has also disappeared, but where these forests remain, there abounds a unique variety of game. A few animals that frequent the lowlands are also common in the midlands (leopard, wild boar, and barking deer).

Himalayan Black Bear (Selenarctos thibetanus)- Kalo Bhalu

The Asiatic black bear is medium-sized (225-400

◀*A wild dog*

lbs.) with smooth fur which is moderate in length. The hair on the neck and shoulders forms a long ruff. The colour is shiny black with a prominent white V-shaped mark on the chest. The chin is white and the nose is reddish brown.

These bears are found throughout the central and eastern midlands from 3,000-4,000 m., inhabiting steep forested hillsides. In summer, they are found near tree line (10,000-12,000 ft.) descending to lower valleys (5,000 ft.) in winter, and they even have been reported from the tarai. Asiatic black bears are omnivorous, but they subsist chiefly on fruits, roots, and mast. In the central midlands, they feed on corn and pumpkins, raising havoc with the farmers' fields. It is the most carnivorous of the bears and many living near villages kill sheep and goats and even cattle.

The bears are ill-tempered, and many porters (load carriers) carry scars of their encounters with these scoundrels when they have met face-to-face on narrow mountain trails. Mating season is usually autumn with cubs produced late in the winter or early in the spring. The young, usually 2 or more, remain with the female for a year or 2.

Clouded Leopard (Neofelis nebulosa)- Dhuwase or Ajingare Chituwa

The clouded leopard has a long body and tail and short limbs. The dorsal pelage varies from gray or earthy brown to pale or yellowish brown. The underparts are white or pale tawny. Large oval or elongate blotches are found on the back and flanks. The limbs and underparts are spotted. A large male, head and body with tail, will measure over 6 ft. (180 cm.) and weigh 40-45 lbs. (18-20 kg.). The canine teeth are exceptionally long.

Clouded leopards inhabit the dense temperate forests of the middle Himalaya between 1,500 and 2,200 meters. They range from Nepal, Sikkim, Bhutan, into Assam, Burma, and South China and extend eastwards into the Malay countries. These animals are largely aboreal and hunt by night. They feed on a variety of prey including monkey, deer, birds, and livestock. Young are born in hollow trees and the litter size is usually two.

Due to its secretive nature and the rareness of reports, little is known about the status of the clouded leopard in Nepal, but it must be extremely rare.

Barking Deer or Muntjak (Muntiacus muntjak)- Mriga or Ratuwa

Muntjaks are small, high-rumped deer with tusk-like upper canines. Their small antlers consist of a basal brow-tine and a main beam mounted on long, bony pedicles which continue downward as prominent bony ridges on each side of the face, hence the name "ribfaced deer" The colour is bright chestnut above and rufous on the underparts and flanks. The height at the shoulder of adult males is from 20-30 in. and their weight 30-45 lbs. (15-20 kg.).

Barking deer have the greatest altitudinal range of any cervid in Nepal (100-3,3000 m. or 400-11,000 ft.).

They inhabit the moist and dry deciduous forests of the tarai and duns, the evergreen broadleaf forests of the Siwaliks and Mahabharat, and the coniferous forests of the midlands. They are most abundant in the midlands.

Muntjaks are usually solitary and are active in the early morning and late evening. Their loud, dog-like bark can be heard throughout the day. Individuals have been heard to call continuously for over an hour. Their diet consists of grasses and browse, and in the fall, oak mast. Mating takes place in November and December, and 1-2 fawns are dropped in March and April.

Serow (Capricornis sumatraensis)- Thar

The serow is rather lanky in build with long, pointed ears, a dorsal crest or mane on the neck and a short tail. Horns are present in both sexes and are marked with narrow transverse rings. The coat is black or gray above and somewhat grizzled because the pelage is whitish at the base. The head and neck are black, fading into rusty red on the shoulders, flanks and lower thighs. The inside of the limbs and belly is dirty gray. There is a varying amount of white on the muzzle, throat, and chest. The height at the shoulder is 35-45 (100 to 110cm) in. and the weight 170-230 lbs. (80-110 kg.).

Serows inhabit densely thicketed ravines, bamboo thickets, and rocky outcroppings in the midlands from 900-3,500 m. They rest in caves beneath overhanging rocks. Males are generally solitary with immatures banding together in herds of 5-15. They feed in early morning and late evening. Their diet consists of shrubs, grasses, and mosses. They often emerge from dense bamboo thickets to sun themselves on large rocks. They repeatedly use the same area to defecate and large heaps of droppings 25-40 in. deep have been found in bamboo thickets and beneath overhanging rocks. When alarmed, they utter a hissing snort, their call is an alarming whistle. Mating commences in October and 1-2 young are born the following May or June after a gestation period of a little over 7 months.

Goral (Nemorhaedus goral)- ghoral

The goral, related to the serow and takin of the Himalaya, the chamois of Europe, and the Rocky Mountain billy goat of North America, belongs to the goat-antelope family. It resembles the serow in appearance, but the goral is smaller in size, lacks facial glands, and has shorter horns. It is goat-like in appearance with stout limbs. The body is covered by a short, wooly undercoat, which is protected by long, coarse guard hairs. Males have a short, semierectile mane. Short horns (5-6 in.) present in both sexes are directed backward and slightly downward. The colour is a darkish golden brown speckled with black to gray or fawn gray. There is a white patch on the throat and a black tip on the tail. The shoulder height is 26-28 in. and the weight 45-70 lbs. (20-30 kg.).

Gorals inhabit the rugged, grassy outcroppings and rocky cliffs near forests in the Mahabharat range midlands from 1,000-2,500 m. They associate in small family groups of 4-8.

They feed in early morning and late evening, spending the day bedded down on nearly inaccessible rocky ledges. The diet consists of forbs, grasses, and mosses. When frightened , they utter a whistling snort. With a gestation period of about 6 months, usually a single kid is born during May or June.

CHAPTER FIVE

Some Wildlife of the Highlands

The highlands or Greater Himalayas comprise the zone of highest elevation with towering, snow-covered peaks. In this region, elevated plateaus and high mountain ranges are separated from one another by great depressions. The highlands rise abruptly north of the midlands, forming a steep, rugged barrier along Nepal's northern border. Most agriculture occurs below this zone, so that about 2,700 m. (9,000 ft.) one finds forests of hemlocks, firs, rhododendrons, and birches. The tree line varies to some degree and usually ends at about 3,900 m. (13,000 ft.)

North of the Greater Himalayan Range, in the districts of Dolpo, Manang, and Mustang, one finds a high alpine desert, unique of the Tibetan Plateau proper. Strong winds blow continuously throughout this near-desert landscape, and this region is largely devoid of vegetation except for a few scraggly junipers and willows and patches of xerophytic, thorny brush. Reduced rainfall combined with high altitude allows Tibetan species to flourish here.

Snow Leopard or Ounce (Panthera uncia)- Him Chituwa

The snow leopard has an elongate body and limbs.

It has a distinctive, short muzzle, a high forehead, and a vertical chin. The fur is long, dense, and woolly. The dorsal colour is a very pale whitish gray, sometimes with a yellowish tinge, and the belly and flanks are white. A pattern of indistinct rosettes occurs on the back and flanks. The thick, furry tail is more than three-quarters the length of the head and body. The ounce is somewhat smaller than a leopard and weighs 60-90 lbs. (25-40 kg.).

The snow leopard is found throughout the Dolpa, Mustang, and Manang Districts and the northern areas of the Greater Himalaya from 3,000-5,000 m. (10,000-16,000 ft.). Generally avoiding forested areas, they seek refuge in rocky crags and ravines. They usually hunt at night, preying on blue sheep, musk deer, Tibetan hares, marmots, larger birds, and livestock. Snow leopards follow the downward migration of animals, moving from high alpine valleys to the fringes of birch-coniferous forests in winter. The gestation period is about 93 days, and the number of young per litter is usually 2-4.

The inaccessibility of their haunts makes observation difficult. Therefore, little is known about this elusive denizen of the High Himalaya. Snow leopards are persistently sought after and hunted for their luxuriant and beautiful fur.

Musk Deer (Moschus moschiferus)- Kasturi Mriga

Musk deer are the most primitive of all living deer. They are robust in build with an elevated rump and a very short tail. They differ from all other deer in that a gall bladder is present. Antlers are lacking in both sexes and males have elongated upper canine teeth 2-3 in. in length, which extend far below the upper lips. Males possess large caudal and preputeal glands or "musk pods." The coat of brittle, hollow hairs is coarse and thick. A large male may weigh 25-35 lbs. (10-12 kg.).

Musk deer are found throughout the subalpine and alpine regions of the midlands and the highlands and also in the alpine desert region of Mustang District. They inhabit rhododendron, coniferous, and birch forests and are found at high elevations (2400-4500 m.) along the base of rocky outcroppings and in bamboo thickets. Solitary in habit, they are active in early morning and late evening. Their diet consists of grasses, mosses, lichens, and alpine flowers. Mating takes place in December or January. The gestation period is about 160 days and a single young, rarely two, is born sometime in June.

Heavy poaching has eliminated the musk deer over much of its original range. The "musk pod" is worth more per gram than gold. Musk is used in perfumes and as an aphrodisiac. The teeth are commonly worn as necklaces by the native peoples in Mugu District. The Chinese have musk deer farms and extract the musk surgically without killing the animal

Yak (Bos grunniens) Nyak

The wild yak is massive in build with short, stout limbs. The withers form a conspicuous hump. The large, black horns curve upward and forward in males and measure 25-35 in. in length. Long mats of hair fringe the lower parts of the shoulder flanks and thighs. The long bushy tail drags the ground. The wild yak bull is nearly twice as large as the domestic variety, standing 2 m. at the shoulder and weighing 1000-1300 lbs. (450-500 kg.)

Strictly a creature of the Tibetan Plateau, they are found in the desolate mountains and alpine steppes of the Dolpa and Mustang Districts. They feed on grass, moss, lichens, and small shurbs. Yaks are called the "grunting ox" because of their deep guttural grunt. When irritated, they grunt and swish their tail vigorously.

Mating takes place in October and November and one calf, rarely two, is born the following April or May. The gestation period is about 10 months. The wild yak has been almost entirely eliminated from Nepal through poaching and hybridization with domestic stock. The hydrid is called chauri.

Himalayan Tahr (Hemitragus jemlahicus)- Jharal

The Himalayan tahr is about 100 cm tall and resembles the true goat (genus Capra), but differs in that both sexes lack a beard. Both sexes have short, laterally compressed horns of about 30 to 40 cm length (10-15 in). in length) which curve backward. Females have 4 mammae instead of 2 as in goats. The colour of the buck is a rich reddish or dark brown. The mane is often lighter, a honey brown, while the face and the front of the legs are dark or blackish brown.

Distributed throughout the Himalayas, they frequent precipitous terrain of the midlands and highlands; from dense broad-leaved forests to steep, alpine mountain slopes between 2000 and 4500 m. (7000-14,000 ft.). they spend much of their time above timberline during summer and autumn.

Like most members of goat family, they are gregarious, traveling in herds of 15-30. Males and females separate in late summer and rejoin in the fall. They are extremely wary and difficult to approach, especially from below. Their principal food is grass, supplemented with browse. Mating takes place between October and January, and females produce their first young at the age of three. The gestation period is about 6-5 months and young are born during May and June. Usually a single young is born, but twins are not uncommon.

Blue Sheep (Pseudois nayaur)- Bharal or Nawar

The bharal is often regarded as an aberrant sheep with goat-like affinities. It is sheep-like in that it lacks a beard and any "goat" smell, but in nearly every other aspect, it resembles the goat family. The back and sides are metallic gray or slate gray in colour, the underparts are white. Males have black markings on the face, chest and sides and a dark stripe down the front of all limbs. Horns, borne by both sexes, are 55-70 cm. (20-30 in.) in length. Peculiar in shape, the horns are rounded and smooth, curving backward over the neck. They stand about 36 in. (90 cm.) at the shoulder and weigh 60-75 kg. (130-170 lb.).

Blue sheep inhabit the Greater Himalayan Range

from treeline to snowline (3600-5000 m.) frequenting steep cliffs and grassy alpine slopes near rocky outcoppings. They are especially plentiful in the far northwestern region (Humla, Jumla, Dolpo and Mustang Districts) of the country bordering Tibet. They usually flock together in herds of 10-30 although up to 300 animals may assemble at times. Herd structure changes with the season with males tending to separate from the females after rut. However, a few young males associate with the females throughout the year.

Their diet consists of grasses, legumes, forbs, ferns, browse and lichens are the main stable of their winter diet. Bharal rut between September and October. After a gestation period of about 160 days, lambs (usually twins) are born from April through June.

Great Tibetan Sheep or Hodgson's Big-Horn Sheep (Ovis ammon hodgsoni)- Nayan

Rams have massive spiral horns 35-50 in. (90-145 cm.) in length, while ewes have only slightly curved horns a few centimeters in length. It is possible to determine the age of a nayan by counting the growth rings on the horns. One growth ring is laid down for each winter after the first year.

The Nayan is the largest of all wild sheep, standing 48 in. (120cm.) at the shoulder and weighing 300-400 lbs. (135-175 kg.). The coat is short, coarse and very close to the body. A large throat ruff is present and a crest of hairs, not as long as the throat ruff, extends from the nape to the withers. The colour is grayish brown above and paler or whitish below. The rump, throat, chest, and inner sides of the legs are white. A dark stripe extends down the front of each leg.

Nayans rarely range south of the Greater Himalayan axis, inhabiting the bare, undulating Tibetan Plateau from Northern Kashmir to Bhutan. Occasionally, they stray into the northern border areas of Nepal frequenting open, rocky alpine meadows between 3500 and 5500 m. (11000-17000 ft.). These sheep are migratory in habit, spending the summer months high in the mountains (5000 m.) descending to lower valleys (3500 m.) during winter.

During summer, rams separate from the ewes and lambs, but band back together during the winter months. Nayan occur in flocks of 15-35 animals. Grasses, flowers, mosses, lichens, and some browse make up their diet. Mating commences in October and lambs are born the following May and June . The gestation period is 150-180 days after which 1-2 lambs are born. The life expectancy in the wild is about 10-15 years.

A roaring tiger ▶

Centre Spread :

A female rhinoceros with a young one

CHAPTER SIX

The Importance of Wildlife Conservation

◀ *An Indian Roller or blue jay*

The forests hold an attraction not only for those interested in hunting, but also for those who wish to enjoy nature. The jungles and forests provide a refreshing and exhilarating change from the artificialities of cities and modern life. As a cure for this strange malady of modern living in Nepal, the potential of wildlife preserves and sanctuaries has to be fully exploited as in the West. Forest recreation does not merely imply facilities for people to see protected wild animals but also the prospects the forests offer for camping and the enjoyment of "nature" in all its aspects. The kaleidoscopic view of the changing landscape compiled of terraced hills, snow-capped mountains, raging rivers, and emerald lakes with constant variations in the floral colours afford a real and lasting thrill to all partakers.

Nature conservations and nature worship were highly valued in ancient Nepali culture. Ancient Sanskrit literature abounds in descriptions of "Topovana" or "the penance forest" as a centre of meditation and education; a means of escape from the worries and anxieties of everyday life and as a perennial source of mental peace and happiness.

The ancient concept of the "Tapovana" as a full-fledged seat of learning is now out-of-date since Nepalese no longer live in a pastoral age.

Here is, for example a poetic description of a *Tapovana*, or a penance forest from the Sanskrit drama *Swapnvasvadatta*, written by Bhasa about the third or the fourth century B.C.: "Deer graze undisturbed because of the trust engendered by the surroundings; trees with branches full of flowers and fruits are tenderely protected; tawny cattle abound and no cultivated and furrowed land is to be seen in any directions. It must be a penance forest because from the routine ritualistic fire is the shelter and protection of many."

The quatrain in Sanskrit runs as follows:

विस्रब्धं हरिणाश्चरन्त्यन्वकिता देशागत प्रत्यया।
वृक्षाः पुष्फलैः समृद्धविरपाः सर्वे दयारक्षिताः
भूयि कपिलानि गोकुल धनान्य क्षत्रवत्या दिशो
सनिग्धनिंद तपोवनमयं धूमेहि वह्वाश्रयः।।

The aforementioned drama also contains a touching description of an evening or sunset in a penance forest: "Birds have roosted in their nests; the ascetic has already taken a dip in the water; fire lit in the open air casts a flickering glow, and the smoke wanders over the penance forest. The sun also, deflecting its course from a distance, has run short of its light or rays and turned back its chariot and also entered the Mount of Setting."

The quatrain in Sanskrit runs as follows:

खगा वासोपेताः सलिलमवगाढ़ो मुनिजनः।
प्रदीप्रोडग्निर्भाति प्रविवरति धूमो मुनिवनम।
परिभ्रष्टो दूराद्रविरपि संक्षिप्त किरणों
रथं व्यावर्न्यासौपतिशति शनैरस्त शिखरम्।।

But the forests can still serve as a first hand source

of knowledge to the students and teachers of botany and zoology from the secondary school stage to the university level. Despite the importance attached to the forests and wildlife in our ancient culture, present interest has suffered a serious decline. Our current attitude towards the forests and wildlife is characterized by a spirit of utter callousness. Only the poachers of game and the timber contractors with their purely destructive intent are interested in the forests, if we are to exclude the land-hungry peasants who have also made considerable inroads on the forest-wealth of the country.

One of the best ways of conserving nature is to make the common people aware of their natural treasures. In the United States, over 50 million people annually visit 33 national parks, with Yellowstone National Park drawing well over 1 million people. In India, where wildlife tourism is in its infancy, Kanha, its most rewarding national park in Madhya Pradesh in 1969, attracted only 79 foreign and 6,603 Indian visitors.

In Nepal, protected areas have recently been established, but they have failed to generate wide popular interest. The Nepali themselves do not seem to be enthusiastic about wildlife reserves. In order to create popular interest in parks and protected areas, information concerning these protected areas must be made readily available to the public. Today transportation and accommodations can be easily provided and widely advertised. Riding elephants should be provided and observation-towers set up at strategic watering holes or game crossings. Salt-licks can also be provided to lure large herbivores within range of these towers. Guides and trackers should be employed so that sanctuaries might attract crowds of visitors. Visitor Centres can provide information and slide shows to educate the public. All this may encourage tourist-oriented business such as transport, nature photography, catering and camping arrangements to flourish.

As a rule, visitors to sanctuaries will be interested in viewing the exotics: tigers, rhinos, leopards and deer. But once a genuine interest is aroused among the ordinary people and students through the encouragement of educational and recreational tours, much else to attract popular interest will be found. Giant flying squirrels, scaly anteaters, horn bills and many other unique creatures may prove to be a source of abiding interest and pleasure to visitors.

Bird Watching

Who does not enjoy watching birds: the picturesqueness of their forms and colours, their buoyant and floating motion in the air and the pleasing qualities of their songs. It is for these reasons that birdwatching novices, with little scientific training, have contributed immensely to our knowledge of the lives and behavior of birds. For a small country, Nepal has a vast avifaunal wealth consisting of about 850 species and subspecies of bird.

In Nepal, birds abound everywhere: on the floor of the jungle, among low bushes, on the trunks of trees, and high in the top of the leafy forest canopy. One notices a rich variety of birds: babblers, birds of prey, treepies, drongoes, fly-catchers, minivets plus numerous other species. These mixed groups of birds are a distinctive feature of Nepal's forests both in the hills and in the plains.

There is nothing like a lake or jheel in the tarai for watching birds in the winter. It is quite an experience to drift along in a dug-out canoe over the tranquil water on a cold morning amidst the honking of geese, the quacking of ducks and the trumpeting of storks while innumerable other varieties of waterfowl and wader (wading bird) flutter and swish all around overhead. The sight of this vast multitude of birds suddenly bursting into a hurried state of activity will leave a lasting impression even on the mind of a casual on-looker.

In the higher altitudes, the impeyan pheasant which is Nepal's national bird is found in the open and steep slopes. Unforgettable is the sight of the 'nine-coloured' pheasant flying down an open grassy slope with its wings of bright metallic hue fully stretched. The early morning flights of hornbills across a riverbed and the distinctive staccato of the generally "invisible cuckoo" and the constant racket of the brain fever bird (hawk-cuckoo or paphiha) are some of the most memorable sights and sounds of the Nepali jungle and forest.

In Nepal, there are many different kinds of birds that are beautiful to watch. The spiny babbler is the pride of Nepal because it does not occur anywhere else in the world. Birds roam about in Nepal according to the season. The sky resounds in spring with the trills, whistles, and chirps when birds are building their nests and rearing young. Many Nepali birds winter in India and return the following spring. Others, considered native, dwell in Nepal the year round. Still others migrate to Nepal from the plateau of Central Asia.

The pioneer avifaunal studies in Nepal were carried out by B.H. Hodgson who resided in Kathmandu for 25 years (1822-1847). His bird collections totalled well over 20,000 skins consisting of 658 species representing several new families, over 20 new genera, and 179 new species. The foremost authorities on Nepalese birds are Drs. Robert L. Fleming, Mr. Robert L. Fleming Sr. and Jr., who had resided in Kathmandu for nearly 3 decades. The Flemings have collected one of the most extensive series of birds, from Nepal and the Himalaya. The Flemings have collected close to 850 species and sub-species from Nepal. Their labours and research knowledge on the bird life of Nepal is contained in their excellent book, *Birds of Nepal*. Without their indefatigable and dedicated efforts, this last remaining avifaunal frontier would not have been successfully conquered.

For one interested in seeing as many different birds as possible, take a trek going from low to high elevations. A three-week trek through the hinterlands of Nepal should produce a bird list of between 300-400 species. Several treks offer a fine introduction to Nepal's bird life. Among these, the Solukhumbu (Everest) area offers spectacular mountains along with high altitude birds. The Kali Gandaki trail to Jomoson affords one the opportunity to see Tibetan species of birds. The Helambu and Langtang routes allow the viewing of snow partridge, tragopans, and impeyan pheasants. The impeyan or Dafe, Nepal's national bird is found in the open and steep slopes of the Himalaya. Unforgettable is the sight of the multicoloured Dafe gliding down an open grassy slope with its wings of bright metallic hue glistening in the sun.

The following description by the Sanskrit poet Bhasa, of the flight of egrets in the evening or the late afternoon on the way to their nests cannot be surpassed in the poetic effect and the aptness of similes: "The line or the row of the cattle egrets in flight with empty spaces interspersed between them in straight, extended and even, and in its turnings, gets crooked like the Constellation of Seven Stars. It casts off a slough, as white as the underbelly of snake, which tends, as it were, to delimit or demarcate the boundary-line of the sky."

The above lines reveal the poet's keen interest in bird watching which must have yielded pleasure to many in his days as now.

The Sanskrit quatrain is given below:

ऋज्वायतां च विरलां नतोनूतां च।
सप्रर्षि वंशकुटिलां च निवर्ततेषु।।
विमुच्यमान भुजगोदरनिर्मलस्य।
सीमामिमाम्बर तलस्य विभज्यमानः।

CHAPTER SEVEN

National Parks and Conservation in Nepal

The national parks movement in Nepal is one aspect of a comparatively new approach to man's relationship with his environment, which throughout history he has always tended to misuse and often to destroy. Paradoxically, the first effective attempts to conserve nature were made by sportsmen. Hunting in Nepal has always been practised as a recreation by the ruling class and it was clearly not in their best interests to see the disappearance of the quarry which gave them their special joy. Preservation of the quarry also meant the preservation of the environment, so from the earliest times, we found the Ranas establishing large areas of the forest as game preserves or shooting blocks exclusively reserved for themselves. These reserved forests were primarily created for the killing of the game animals they contained, but they also incidentally served to protect the flora and all the other animals in the forest.

Ranging from the subtropical forests of the tarai to the great peaks of the Himalaya in the north, Nepal can boast some of the most spectacular natural areas in all of Asia. Between these extremes, one finds very vegetational type from the treeless steppes of the trans-Himalayan region in the extreme north, the birch, silver fir, larch and hemlock of the highlands to the oak, pine and rhododendron forests of the midlands, to the great sal forests of the lowlands.

The rolling, densely forested hills and broad dun valleys of the lowlands were once renowned for the abundance and variety of wildlife. Though much depleted as a result of agricultural settlements, deforestation, poaching and overgrazing, this region of Nepal still boasts a richer and more varied fauna than any other area in South Asia. Though the loss of irreplaceable vegetation and the wildlife these forests support is a tragedy in itself, this is by no means the only consideration. There are few regions in the world where conservation of the natural environment is of more crucial importance to mankind. Environmental destruction causes mountain slides in the higher Himalayan valleys and with it, the landslides, soil erosion, floods, loss of topsoil, and silting of major river ecosystems depriving food and energy supplies for the people living there.

The fauna and flora of the region comprises an important part of Nepal's natural and cultural heritage. Conservation and management of these unique ecosystems together with the indigenous fauna and flora is of utmost importance both ecologically and economically. The creation of National Parks and reserves in Nepal is justified by their considerable recreational, educational and scientific importance. It is necessary to ensure the conservation of the forests and wildlife so that they may be handed on to future generations. As in other parts of the world, it may be "too little too late" in the case of Nepal.

To make conservation management of the country's valuable but fast diminishing wildlife resource a reality, His Majesty's Government (HMG) of Nepal initiated a National Parks and Wildlife Conservation Project in collaboration with the Food and Agricultural Organisation/United Nations Development Programme (FAO/UNDP) in 1973. Initially, this project has provided effective conservation and management of Nepal's dwindling wildlife including their habitats. This has played an important role in the growing tourist industry and at the same time has provided the needed environmental protection

Within 20 years of its inception, Nepal has been able to establish 8 national parks and 4 wildlife reserves in representative areas of unique and fragile ecosystems. The present programme also envisions the extension of the existing parks and reserves. The existing national parks and reserves are: (1) the Royal Chitawan National Park, (2) the Royal Bardia National Park (3) the Khaptad National Park (4) Rara National Park, (5) the Shey-Phaksoundo National Park (6) the Langtang National Park (7) the Mount Everest (Sagarmatha) National Park, (8) the Makalu- Barune National Park (9) the Koshi Tapu Wildlife Reserve, (10) the Parsa Wildlife Reserve (11) Shivapuri Wildlife Reserve and (12) the Sukla Phanta Wildlife Reserve. The Annapurna Conservation Area and Makalu Barun Conservation Area are two new catagories of Protected areas.

These parks and reserves cover approximately 14% of Nepal and Shey Phaksoundo (Dolpo) National Park is the largest one with 3,555 Sq Km area.

Limited space will permit us only to present a cursory overview of an existing national park and wildlife reserve.

Lantang National Park

Lantang is the second largest of Nepal's eight existing national parks covering ca.1,710 sq. km. (660 sq. mi.). The park is situated in the central Himalayan region, and its southern border lies about 30 km. north of Kathmandu. To the west, its boundary follows the Bhote Kosi-Trisuli Ganga (river), and to the north and east, the boundary follows the Nepal-China border. The park lies within portions of Rasuwa, Nuwakot, and Sindu Palchok Districts. The creation of a national park in this area has come none too soon from a conservation viewpoint, as problems of human impact are already paramount.

Lantang is the most accessible of the mountain parks and can be reached throughout the year by a combination of motor transport and trekking (hiking). A popular route from Kathmandu is by jeep or bus to Dhunche or Sabrubeshi via Trisuli Bazaar and then trekking for about 5 days to Lantang Valley. Alternative routes are from Sundarijal or Panchkhal, northwards over Gosainkunda or Gangya La Pass. A STOL airstrip at Chhong Du, in the upper Langtang Valley, is suitable for light aircraft and could be easily improved to accommodate Twin Otters.

The park, regarded as part of the Central Himalaya, is bisected east-west by the Gosainkunda Lekh-Dorje

Lhakpa Range. North of the Lantang Khola (river) Lantang Lerung Peak (7,245 m or 23,771 ft.) dominates the Lantang Himal, while to the southeast lies the Gosain Kunde Lekh (mountain range). The deeply bisected terrain of the park encompasses an altitudinal range of over 6,450 m. (21,170 ft.) extending from upper tropical forests to permanent snow and ice fields. The area is particularly interesting for its wide variety of vegetation: *Rhododendron* sp., *Larix nepalensis* and *Picea smithiana*. The climate is typically monsoonal, though north of the Gosainkunda Range, there is a rainshadow effect.

Birds abound and there are some 160 species found within the park. There are also a number of unique mammals found within the area: lesser or red panda, wild dog, leopard, musk deer, serow, goral, and jharal (Himalayan tahr). About 45 villages occur within the park together with numerous other settlements adjacent to its boundary. These depend on the park's natural resources for their livelihood. The region is already popular with trekkers; 5000 to 7000 tourists visit the park annually and this number will increase in the near future.

Royal Bardia National Park

The Royal Bardia National Park was formerly gazetted as a Wildlife Reserve in 1976 with an area of 386 sq km. In 1988 it was made a national park with an extended area of 968 sq. km. including Babai Valley. Formerly a Royal Shikar (hunting) Reserve, it supports an unusually rich variety of wildlife and is one of the main strongholds of the tiger and gharial or fish-eating

crocodile (*Gavialis gangeticus*). This reserve includes a section of the Gerwa River (the eastern branch of the Karnali downstream of its gorge) and the Chure (Siwalik) hills, but the bulk of the reserve consists of fairly flat, alluvial land under dense sal forests.

The park is located in southwestern Nepal 396 km. (248 mi.) west of Kathmandu (81° 20' E, 28° 35'N). The whole of the park lies in Bardia and Banke Districts of the Bheri Zone. The Gerwa River, a branch of the Karnali, forms the western boundary. The crest of the Chure hills delineates the northern boundary with Nepalganj Surkhet Highway forming the eastern boundary. For the most part, the park consists of flat, forested land lying between 152 and 304 m. (500-1,000 ft.) . Rainfall is moderately high, about 1,500 mm. or 60 in. annually. The land is well-drained by a number of rivers which rise in the Chure and flow to the southwest or tributaries of the Karnali. The river islands and other riverine areas are forested by distinct riverine associations—mixed deciduous and semideciduous broadleaf trees.

Access to the park is through Mahendra Highway (Kohalpur- Banbasa Section). A feeder road from Mahendra Highway joins Thakurdwara park Headquarter.

Historically, the area was afforded some measure of protection as a hunting ground. In retrospect, it has remained one of the richer pockets of wildlife while other areas of the tarai have been heavily exploited. Nowhere west of Chitawan District is there known to be a greater variety of wildlife in such an attractive

stretch of relatively unspoiled country. The great Karnali River has no equal in Nepal and the wealth of fish *e.g., the mahseer Tor (Barbus-tor)* and the presence of gharial, mugger crocodiles, and Gangetic dolphin add enormously to the importance of the area in the scheme of natural conservation. The reserve will also play a vital role in the survival of the barasingha or swamp deer and the black buck antelope. Other endangered and threatened wildlife found in the reserve are the dhole or Asiatic wild dog, wild elephant, leopard and tiger. Presently rhinoceros has been translocated here from Chitawan.

The Future

Even though the future may look bleak for wildlife in Nepal due to the destruction of prime wildlife habitat, population pressure for new agricultural lands, overgrazing, and poaching, at least a start has been made in the right direction. It is not only Nepal's responsibility, but the entire environmental community of the world, to preserve these unique and fragile ecosystems along with their precious fauna and flora. Nepal still has a long way to go in order to save its forests and wildlife.

Field surveys should be carried out and monitoring stations set up to fulfill the aims and objectives of the existing parks and reserves. There should be proposed extensions of the existing parks to save critical wildlife habitat from further destruction. There should be surveys of new areas conducted for possible inclusion into national parks and reserves

There should be training courses for wildlife personnel to upgrade the management system of the national parks and wildlife conservation. Tourism should be promoted in the parks to help furnish a source of revenue. Conservation education programmes should be instituted to educate the general public. The introduction of visitor interpretative centres at the existing parks should be instituted. Booklets, pamphlets and posters on the wildlife forests, and national parks should be distributed to the local people. Further major research projects such as the Tiger Ecology Project in conjunction with His Majesty's Government, the King Mahendra Trust for Nature Conservation and World Wildlife Fund should be encouraged. And efforts should be made to generate more additional funds for wildlife management and habitat preservation through bilateral, international, voluntary, and non-governmental agencies.

Only then will the deterioration of the forests and the destruction of the wildlife be halted, and hopefully be reversed.

Appendices

APPENDIX A

Areas of National Parks and Protected Areas

	Area in Sq. Km.
1. National Parks	
Chitawan	932
Royal Bardia	968
Sagarmatha	1,148
Langtang	1,710
Rara	106
Shey-Phoksundo (Dolpa)	3,555
Khaptad	225
Makalu-Barun	1,500
	10,144
2. Wildlife Reserve	
Royal Suklaphanta	155
Parsa	500
Koshitappu	175
Sivapuri Watershed	145
3. Dhorpatan Hunting Reserve	1,325
4. Makalu-Barun Conservation Area	830
	Total - 13,274

Percentage of Protected Areas - 9%
Above listing does not include Annapurna Conservation Area which is about 2600 sq.km.

Source: B.N. Upreti (1993)

APPENDIX B

Protected Wildlife Species of Nepal

Mammals	Scientific names
Assames rhesus monkey	Macaca assamensis
Pangolin	Manis crassicaudata and M. pentadactyla
Hispid hare	Capralagus hispidus
Gangetic dolphin	Platanista gangetica
Wolf	Canis lupus
Himalayan black bear	Selenarctos thibetanus
Red panda	Ailurus fulgens
Spotted linsang	Prionodon pardicolor
Hyena	Hyeana hyeana
Leopard cat	Felis bengalensis
Lynx	Felis lynx
Clouded leopard	Neofelis nebulosa
Tiger	Panthera tigris
Snow leopard	Panthera uncia
Wild Elephant	Elephas maximus
Rhinoceros	Rhinoceros unicornis
Pygmy hog	Sus salvanius
Musk deer	Moschus moschiferus
Swamp deer	Cervus duvauceli
Gaur bison	Bos gaurus
Wild Yak and nyak	Bos grunniens
Wild buffalo	Bubalus bubalis
Wild sheep or nayan	Ovis ammon hodgsoni
Tibetan antelope	Pantholops hodgsoni
Blackbuck	Antelope cervicapra
Four horned antelope	Tetracerus quadricornis

Birds	
Black stork	Ciconia nigra
White stork	Ciconia ciconia
Sarus crane	Grus antigone
Impeyan pheasant or Daphe	Lophophorus impejanus
Cheer pheasant	Catreus wallichii
Crimson horned pheasant	Tragopan satyra
Bengal florican	Euphodotis bengalensis
Lesser florican	Sypheotides indica
Giant hornbill	Buceros bicornis
Reptiles	
Python	Python species
Gharial crocodile	Gavialis gangeticus
Yellow monitor lizard	Varanus flavescens

Source B.N. Upriti (1993)

APPENDIX C

A Checklist of Common Nepali Mammals

Common Name	Scientific Name	Nepali Name
Anteater, Scaly or Pangolin	*Manis pentadactyla*	Salak
Antelope, Black Buck	*Antilope cervicapra*	Krishna-Sar or Barat
Antelope, Four Horned	*Tetracerus Quadricornis*	Chausingha
Blue Bull	*Boselaphas tragocamelus*	Nilgai or Ghod Gada
Bear, Himalayan Black	*Selenarctos thibetanus*	Kalo Bhalu
Bear, Sloth	*Melurus ursinus*	Bhalu
Badger, Honey or Ratel	*Mellivora capensis*	Khude Kiro
Boar, Wild	*Sus scrofa*	Badel
Buffalo, Wild	*Bubalus bubalis*	Arna
Cat, Fishing	*Felis viverrina*	Machha Marne Biralo
Cat, Golden	*Felis temmincki*	Sunaula Biralo
Cat, Jungle	*Felis chaus*	Ban Biralo
Cat, Leopard	*Felis bengalensis*	Chituwa Biralo/ Charibagh
Cat, Marbled	*Felis marmorata*	Marble Biralo
Civet, Himalayan Palm	*Paguma larvata*	Himali Kasturi Biralo
Civet, Palm or Toddy Cat	*Paradoxurus hermophroditus*	Toddy Biralo
Civet, Large Indian	*Viverra zibetha*	Thulo Hind Civet or Khadot
Civet, Small Indian	*Viverricula indica*	Sano Hind Civet
Dog, Wild or Dhole	*Cuon alpinus*	Jangali Kukur
Deer, Barking	*Muntiacus muntjak*	Mriga or ratua
Deer, Hog	*Axis porcinus*	Laguna
Deer, Musk	*Moschus moschiferus*	Kasturi
Deer, Spotted	*Axis axis*	Chittal
Deer, Swamp	*Cervus duvauceli*	Barasingha
Dolphin	*Platanista gangetica*	Sos

Elephant	*Elephas maximus*	Hati
Fox, common	*Vulpes bengalensis*	Phyauro
Fox, Red	*Vulpes vulpes*	Rato Phyauro
Gaur	*Bos gaurus*	Guri Gai
Hyena	*Hyaena hyaena*	Hundar
Goral	*Nemorhaedus goral*	Ghoral
Hog, Pigmy	*Sus salvanius*	Bam-pudke -Banel
Hare,	*Lepus nigricollis*	Kharayo
Jackal	*Canis aureus*	Shyal
Leopard	*Panthera pardus*	Chituwa
Leopard, Clouded	*Neofelis Nebulosa*	Dhuwase or Ajingare Chituwa
Leopard, Snow or Ounce	*Panthera uncia*	Him Chituwa
Marten	*Martes flavigula*	Malsapro
Marmot, Himalayan	*Marmota bobak*	Himali Marmot
Mongoose Common	*Herprstes edwardsi*	Newuri musa
Monkey, Langur	*Presbytis entellus*	Dhendu
Monkey, Rhesus	*Macaca mulatta*	Banar (Rato)
Otter	*Lutra lutra*	Ot
Pika or Mouse-hare	*Ochotona roylei*	Muse-Kharayo
Procupine, Indian Crested	*Hystrik indica*	Dumsi
Rhinoceros, Indian	*Rhinoceros unicornis*	Gainda
Panda, Lesser or Red	*Ailurus fulgens*	Okrapa Habre
Serow	*Capricornis sumatraensis*	Thar
Sheep, Blue	*Pseudois nayaur*	Bharal/nawar
Sheep, Great Tibetan	*Ovis ammon*	Nayan
Squirrel, Five-lined palm	*Funambulus pennanti*	Lokharke
Squirrel, Orange-bellied	*Dremomys lokriah*	Lokriah
Squirrel, Giant Flying	*Petaurista petaurista* Koiralo	Udne Musa
Tahr, Himalayan	*Hemitragus jemlahicus*	Jharal
Sambar	*Cervus unicolor*	Jarayo
Tiger	*Panthera tigris*	Bagh
Yak, Wild	*Bos grunniens*	Yak, chaurigai

APPENDIX D

A Checklist of Common Nepali Birds

Common Name	Scientific Name	Nepali Name
Dove	*Streptopelia sp.*	Dhukur
Red Turtle Dove	*Streptopelia tranquebarica (Rufous TD)*	Tamoowa Dhukur
Spotted Dove	*Streptopelia chinensis*	Koorle Dhukur
Emerald Dove	*Chalcophaps indica*	Soon Dhukur
Tickell's Thrush	*Turdus unicolor*	Chanchar
Small-billed Mountain Thrush	*Zoothera dauma*	Gobare Chanchar
White-crested Laughing Thrush	*Garrulax leucolophus*	Bhyakura
Whistling Thrush	*Myiophonus calruleus*	Kalchaure
Streaked Laughing Thrush	*Garrulax lineatus*	Suba
White Throated Laughing Thrush	*Garrulax albogularis*	Tori Ghane
Orange-headed Ground Thrush	*Zoothers citrina*	Pattu
Woodpecker	*Dinopium benghalense*	Lache
Wryneck	*Jynx torquilla*	Lahanche
Tree Pie	*Dendrocitta vagabunda*	Kokale
Magpie, Yellow billed	*Kitta flavirostris*	Lampuchchhare
White-checked Bulbul	*Pycnonotus leucogenys*	Jureli
Shrike, Black-headed	*Lanius schach*	Bhadrai
White-collared Blackcird	*Turdus albocinctus*	Kanthe or Kyanki
Grey-headed Myna	*Sturnus malabaricus*	Sarung or Dangre
Wagtail	*Motacilla sp.*	Chweenya
Purple Sunbird	*Nectarinia asiatica*	Boonge-chara
Green Finch	*Carduelis spinoides*	Tori chara
Sparrow	*Passer domesticus*	Bhangera
Magpie Robin	*Copsychus saularis*	Dhobini
White-capped Redstart	*Chaimarrornis leucocephalus*	Pirja
Grey Tit	*Parus major*	Chichinkote

Scarlet Minivet	*Pricrocotus flammeus*	Ranichari
Black Drongo	*Dicrurus adsimilis*	Chibe
Blue Rock Pigeon	*Columba livia*	Parewa, Malewa
Gold-fronted Chloropsis	*Chloropsis aurifrons*	Harewa
Jungle Crow	*Corvus macrorhynchos*	Kalo Kag
House Crow	*Corvus splendens*	Kag
Lark	*Alauda gulgula*	Dhanchari
Black-headed Oriole	*Oriolus xanthornus*	Nyauli
Coppersmith Barbet	*Maegalaima haemacephala*	Kuthurke
Hoopoe	*Upupa epops*	Phapre Charo
Indian Roller	*Coracias benghalensis*	Theua or Nilkanthe
Grey Hornbill	*Tokus birostris*	Dhanesh
Large Indian Parakeet	*Psittacula eupatria*	Suga
The Cuckoo	*Cuculus canorus*	Kuku
Koel Cuckoo	*Endynamys scolopacea*	Koeli
Barn Owl	*Tyto alba*	Lato Kosero
Nightjar	*Caprimulgus asiaticus*	Chaite Chara
Common Swallow	*Hirundo rustica*	Gaunthali
House Swift	*Apus affinis*	Gaunthali
Kingfisher	*Alcedo atthis*	Matokore
Peafowl	*Pavo cristatus*	Majoor
Red Junglefowl	*Gallus gallus*	Luiche
Chir Pheasant	*Catreus wallichi*	Chir
Crimson-horned Pheasant	*Satyra Tragopan*	Monal
Impeyan Pheasant	*Lophophorus impejanus*	Danphe
Black Pheasant	*Lophural leucomelana*	Kalij
Chukor Partridge	*Alectoris graeca*	Chyakhura
Black Partridge	*Francolinus francolinus*	Titra
Snow Partridge	*Lerwa lerwa*	Hiun Titra
Grey Partridge	*Francolinus pondicerians*	Titra
Hill Partridge	*Arborphila torqueola*	Pyura
Quail	*Coturnic coturnix*	Batai
Common Green Pigeon	*Treron phoenicoptera*	Haleso
Woodcock	*Scolopax rusticola*	Bhut-bhute
Stone Curlew	*Burhinus oedicnemus*	Gainde or Dagar
	Batai	

Snow Cock	*Tetraogallus tibetanus*	Komo (Thakali)
King Vulture	*Torgos calvus*	Raj Giddha
Crested Serpent Eagle	*Spilornis cheela*	Kakakool, Chatak
Sarus Crane	*Antigone Grus*	Sarus
Swamp Partridge	*Francolinus gularis*	Teetar
Redwattled Lapwing	*Vanellus indicus*	Huti Tyaun
Yellowwattled Lapwing	*Vanellus malabbricus*	Huti Tyaun
Barheaded Goose	*Anser indicus*	Khoya Hans
Pallas' Fishing Eagle	*Haliaeetus leucoryphus*	Khole Bhaj
Sparrow Hawk	*Accipiter nipisus*	Baj
Common Kite	*Milvus migrans*	Chil
Redlegged Falconet	*Microhierax caerulescens*	Bauri
Spurwinged Plover	*Vanellus spinosus*	Hatityaun
Mallard	*Anas platyrhynchos*	Niltauke Hans or Nil Sar
Common Teal	*Anas Crecca*	Kirkire Hans
Wigeon	*Anas penelope*	Kaude Hans
Ruddy Shelduck or Brahmany Duck	*Tadorna ferruginea*	Chakhewa
Whitenecked Stork	*Ciconia episcopus*	Bhuri phor
Ibis, Black	*Threskiornis melanocephala*	Kanka
Ibis, White	*Pseudibis papillosa*	Lal Sar
Darter or Snake Bird	*Anhinga rufa*	Jal Kaua
Small Egret (Heron)	*Egretta garzetta*	Bakula
Pond Heron	*Ardeola grayii*	Shim Bakula
Cattle Egret	*Bubulcus ibis*	Kalki Bakula
Large Egret	*Egretta abla*	Seto Bakula
Snipe	*Capella gallinago*	Chaha
Common Sand-piper	*Tringa hypoleucus*	Pani Dhukur
Little Ringed Plover	*Charadriius dubius*	Sano Pani Dhukur
Lesser Florican	*Sypheotides indica*	Phakras
Indian River Tern	*Sterna aurantia*	Rammalewa
Demoiselle Crane	*Anthropoides virgo*	Karyangkurung

Nirala Series

A Series of Contemporary Literature

A Prayer in Daylight
Poems
Yuyutsu R.D.

Dying in Rajasthan
Short Stories
Ramanand Rathi
Translated from the Hindi

Elysium in the Halls of Hell
Poems about India
David Ray

Dispossessed Nests
The 1984 Poems
Jayanta Mahapatra

From the Other End
Poems
Banira Giri
Adapted from the Nepali by Yuyutsu R.D.

Hunger of our Huddled Huts
& other Poems
Yuyutsu R.D.

Men Before Fire
& other Poems
Bimal Nibha
Translated from the Nepali by Yuyutsu R.D.

Blackout
A Novel
Taranath Sharma
Translated from the Nepali by Larry Hartsell

The Black Sun
A Novel
Bharat Jungam
Translated from the Nepali

Muna Madan
A Play in the Jhyaure Folk Tradition
Laxmi Prasad Devkota
Translated from the Nepali by Ananda P. Shrestha

Summer Rain
Three Decades of Poetry
K. Satchidanandan
Translated from the Malyalam

Some Female Yeti
& other Poems
Yuyutsu R.D.

Where Laxmi Lies, Caged
& other Stories
Rajendra Yadav
Translated from the Hindi

Conservation
A Drama
Basu Shashi
Translated from the Nepali by Okima Jiunin Gwynn

Roaring Recitals : Five Nepali Poets
(Gopal P. Rimal, Bhupi Sherchan,
Banira Giri, Shailendra Sakar, Bimal Nibha)
Edited & Translated from the Nepali by Yuyutsu R.D.

Fever
Short Stories
Sita Pandey
Translated from the Nepali

Sheet of Snow
An Anthology of Short Stories from the Himalayas
Translated from the Nepali by Nagendra Sharma

In the City of Partridges
Selected Poems
Jagdish Chaturvedi
Translated from the Hindi

Says Meera
An Anthology of Devotional Songs of Meera,
India's Greatest Women Poet
Translated from the Rajasthani by Vijay Munshi

Nirala Series

A Series of Contemporary Writing on Nepal and Buddhism

The Gurkhas
A History of the Recruitment in the British Indian Army
Kamal Raj Singh Rathaur

The Khasa Kingdom
A Trans-Himalayan Empire of the Middle Age
Surya Mani Adhikary

Sources of Inflation in Asia
Theory and Evidences
Raghab D. Pant

The Sherpas : Fire of Himal
An Anthropological Study of the Sherpas of Nepal Himalayan Region
Ramesh Raj Kunwar

A Macro-economic Study of the Nepalese Plan Performance
Gunanidhi Sharma

Folk Culture of Nepal
An Analytical Study
Ram Dayal Rakesh

Fundamentals of Library and Information Science
A Nepalese Response
Madhusudan Sharma Subedi

Transit of Land-locked Countries and Nepal
Gajendra Mani Pradhan

The Gurungs: Thunder of Himal
A Cross-cultural Study of a Nepalese Ethnic Group
Murari P. Regmi

Gods and Mountains:
The Folk Culture of a Himalayan Kingdom: Nepal
Kesar Lall

Folk Tales of Sherpa and Yeti
Shiva Dhakal

Art and Culture of Nepal
An Attempt towards Preservation
Saphalya Amatya

The Dhimals: Miraculous Migrants of Himal
An Anthropological Study of a Nepalese Ethnic Group
Rishikeshab Raj Regmi

Sales Promotion in Nepal
Policies and Practices
Parashar Prasad Koirala

Glimpses of Tourism, Airlines and Management in Nepal
B.R. Singh

The Taming of Tibet
A Historical Account of Compromise and Confrontation in Nepal-Tibet Relations (1900-1930)
Tirtha Prasad Mishra

Dolpo: The Hidden Paradise
A Journey to the Endangered Sanctuary of the Himalayan Kingdom of Nepal
Karna Sakya

Secrets of Shangri-la
An Inquiry into the Lore, Legend and Culture of Nepal
Nagendra Sharma

Indo-Nepal Trade Relations
A Historical Analysis of Nepal's Trade with the British India
Shri Ram Upadhyaya

Politics and Development in Nepal: Some Issues
Narayan Khadka

The Gurkha Connection
A History of Gurkha Recruitment in the British Army
Purshottam Baskota

Lore and Legend of the Kathmandu Valley
Shiva Dhakal

Recent Nepal
The Analysis of the Recent Democratic Upsurge and its Aftermath
Laksman Bahadur K.C.

Popular Deities, Emblems and Images of Nepal
Dhruba K. Deep

Cultural Heritage of Nepal Terai
Ram Dayal Rakesh

The Nepala-mahatmya
Legends on the Sacred Places and Deities of Nepal
Jayaraj Acharya

A Glossary of Himalayan Buddhism
Jagadish Chandra Regmi

Kathmandu, Patan & Bhakatapur
An Archaeological Anthropology of the Royal Cities of the Kathmandu Valley
Rishikeshab R. Regmi

The Himalayan Mind
A Cross-cultural Nepalese Investigation
Murari P. Regmi

Wildlife in Nepal
Rishikesh Shah & Richard M. Mitchell

Politics of Himalayan River Waters
An Analysis of the River Water Issues of Nepal, India and Bangladesh
B.C. Uprety

The Nepali Congress
An Analysis of the Party's Performance in the General Elections and its Aftermath
B.C. Uprety

Nepal-India
Democracy in the Making of Mutual Trust
Dinesh Bhattarai & Pradip Khatiwada

Making of Modern Nepal:
A Study of History, Art and Culture of the Principalities of Western Nepal
Ram Niwas Pandey

Encounter Wildlife in Nepal
Karna Sakya

Constitutional Monarchy and Parliamentary Democracy in Nepal
Laksman Bahadur K.C.

Hindu-Buddhist Festivals of Nepal
Hemanta Kumar Jha

Bhutan : A Movement in Exile
D.N.S. Dhakal & Christopher Strawn

Mountain Dimensions
An Altitude Geographic Analysis of Environment and Development of the Himalayas
Ram Kumar Panday

To the Battlefield on an Elephant
Columns of Fire
Tara Nath Sharma

Nepal: A Concise History of the Cultural Scenario of the Himalayan Kingdom
Jagdish Shumsher Rana

Human Rights in the Hindu-Buddhist Tradition
Lal Deosa Rai

Religious Minorities in Nepal
An Analysis of the State of Buddhists and Muslims in the Himalayan Kingdom
Mollica Dastider

The Questions of Dharma in the Mahabharata
Birendra Mishra

Malla Coins of Medieval Nepal
Jagdish Chandra Regmi

Vishvarupa Mandir
A Study of Changu Narayan, Nepal's most Ancient Temple
Jeff Lidke

New Direction in Nepal-India Relations
Rishikesh Shaha

Tamang Shamans
An Ethnopsychiatric Study of Ecstasy and Healing in Nepal
Larry Peters

Nepal: Missing Elements in the Development Thinking
Dr Gunanidhi Sharma

Ethnic Conflict in Bhutan
Political and Economic Dimensions
Mathew Joseph C.

Rana Rule in Nepal
Saphalya Amatya

Trance, Initiation & Psychotherapy in Nepalese Shamanism
Essays on Tamang & Tibetan Shamanism
Larry G. Peters

The Political Economy of Land, Landlessness and Migration in Nepal
Nanda R. Shrestha

Slavery in Nepal
Dil B. Chetri